THE MONSTER'S BONES

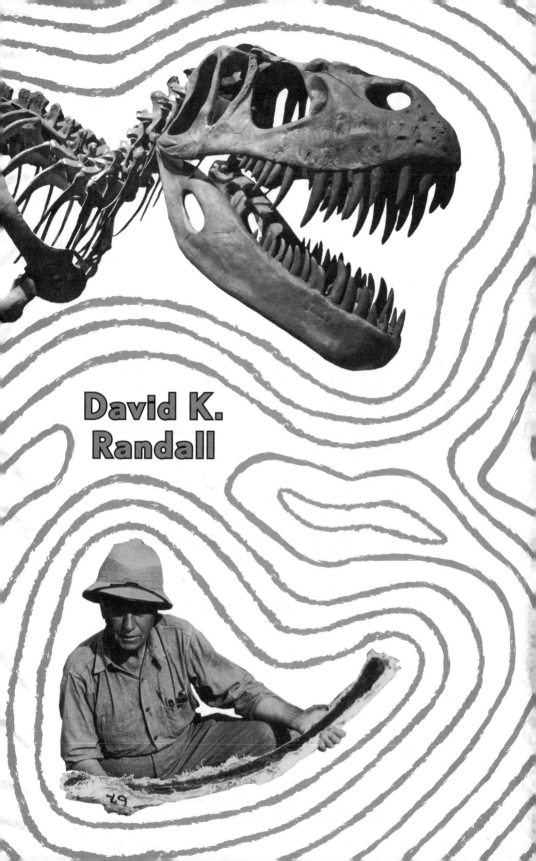

David K. Randall

THE MONSTER'S BONES

YOUNG READERS EDITION

The DISCOVERY of T. REX and HOW IT SHOOK OUR WORLD

Norton Young Readers
An Imprint of W. W. Norton & Company
Celebrating a Century of Independent Publishing

For information about permission to reproduce selections from this book, write to
Permissions, W. W. Norton & Company, Inc., 500 Fifth Avenue, New York, NY 10110

For information about special discounts for bulk purchases, please contact
W. W. Norton Special Sales at specialsales@wwnorton.com or 800-233-4830

Manufacturing by Lake Book Manufacturing
Book design by Hana Anouk Nakamura
Production manager: Delaney Adams

W. W. Norton & Company, Inc., 500 Fifth Avenue, New York, N.Y. 10110
www.wwnorton.com

W. W. Norton & Company Ltd., 15 Carlisle Street, London W1D 3BS

1 2 3 4 5 6 7 8 9 0

To Diane Randall,
who took me to every museum she could.

Nature has a habit of placing some of her most attractive treasures in places where it is difficult to locate and obtain them.

　　—Charles Doolittle Walcott, fourth secretary of
　　　the Smithsonian Institution

Contents

Prologue

THE CENTER OF THE WORLD

Depending on which entrance you choose, the American Museum of Natural History looks like a castle, a sun-bleached Roman temple, or a spaceship ready to launch out of a glass box. The fact that its sides don't match is the first clue that the museum, with its maze of twenty-eight interconnected buildings in the middle of Manhattan, grew organically and mostly by chance. Since its founding in 1869, the museum has gathered, categorized, and displayed all that is amazing, strange, and beautiful about the planet Earth and the universe in which it spins. To tour its collection is to experience the sum of human knowledge of the world surrounding us and our best guesses at how we fit into the picture.

The numbers alone are so large as to seem made up. Among the museum's possessions are nearly 7 million wasps, 3 million butterflies, 1 million birds, and over 2 million fish, though they are no longer swimming. And that's just a modest survey of its extensive library of small animals. If the contents of the museum were taken across the street and laid out in Central Park like a gigantic yard sale, you could have your pick from:

- **the bones of 100 elephants, including the skeleton of Jumbo, once the most famous zoo animal in the world and the reason why the English language gained a new word for something particularly big**
- **one 34-ton meteorite called Ahnighito that is nearly as old as the sun**
- **45 musical instruments from the Congo**

- the stump of a 1,400-year-old sequoia
- 51 balls used in sports ranging from lacrosse to a game played by the Tupari people of South America, in which players could only touch the ball with their heads
- the skeleton of a 3.1-million-year-old hominid woman that scientists named Lucy after a Beatles song that was playing on the radio
- a set of dinosaur footprints that are at least 107 million years old
- a 563-carat blue star sapphire known as the Star of India
- a taxidermized Galapagos tortoise
- a shirt woven by the Cheyenne decorated with locks of human hair
- a 4.5-ton block of azurite—bright blue-and-green malachite ore from Arizona that contains so much copper it can vibrate and hum when the air becomes very humid, giving it the nickname the Singing Stone.

How each wonder of the natural world came to sit in a museum in one of the most densely populated places on Earth is its own story. Yet even with an array of the splendid and surreal, it is no exaggeration to say that most of the 5 million people who visit the museum each year come only because of one specimen: the *Tyrannosaurus rex.* Though the last of its kind died more than 66 million years ago, the massive jaws, tiny forearms, and long teeth of a *T. rex* are as instantly recognizable as the *Mona Lisa* or the Eiffel Tower. It is not every day that one can confront a huge beast that could eat you up in a gulp or two, like the monster from a nightmare made real, should it somehow come back to life.

For thirty years, the museum was the only place in the world where you could view a *T. rex*. More than any other museum specimen, the *T. rex* is quilted into modern culture, found everywhere from clothing to toy stores to blockbuster movies. Its familiarity makes it seem like it has always been with us. Yet there was a time not very long ago when everything about this prehistoric beast was entirely new. Its discovery landed with a thud that shifted our understanding of ourselves—and our planet reverberates still.

THE MONSTER'S BONES

CHAPTER ONE

A LIFE THAT COULD CONTAIN HIM

The boy needed a name.

It was a duty that William and Clara Brown had taken seriously three times before, following the births of their two daughters and a son. Now, with another infant staring up at them in the farmhouse where they lived on the outskirts of Carbondale, Kansas, it seemed an overwhelming task. A name was supposed to guide the child on a safe and righteous path, instilling trust in others and resolve in oneself. But all their good ideas had been taken. Their two daughters, Melissa and Alice, had been named after family, closing off that avenue of inspiration. At the age of six, their first son, Frank, was as forthright as his name suggested, developing into a miniature version of his father. Yet here before them lay another boy, and several days after his birth he still didn't have a name.

Leaving so weighty a decision to the last minute was entirely out of the Brown character. Like all farmers at the mercy of the weather, William prized certainty where he could find it. Born in Virginia in 1833, he migrated to the open plains of the west as a twenty-one-year-old in search of a better chance. In Wisconsin, he met Clara Silver, the fifteen-year-old daughter of a prosperous dairy farmer, and the two were married by the end of the year. They eventually settled in Osage County, in the eastern part of the state near the Missouri border, on a spot named Carbon Hill due to the long bands of coal which blackened the soil.

During the Civil War, William won a richly rewarding contract to lead wagon trains full of supplies for the U.S. Army across the open frontier. Once the war was over, he watched as ribbons of railroad tracks appeared on the plains, stitching together the Transcontinental Railroad and boxing in what had seemed to be the limitless horizon. The rails made him feel like a relic in his own time. Determined not to be left further behind, he entered the mining business, using his team of oxen to clear off the topsoil of his land and uncover bands of coal that could be extracted from the earth. Though never rich by the standards of a city, the Browns grew prosperous enough that they employed thirty-one men to help run the farm and dig up coal, feeding everyone three times a day in the family's living room. With any money that was left over, they traveled up to the capital city of Topeka and its diversions.

It was there that six-year-old Frank saw an advertisement for P. T. Barnum's Great Traveling World's Fair plastered on barns, trees, and the sides of office buildings. Soon he could think of nothing but the circus. After the birth of his younger brother a month later on February 12, 1873, William and Clarissa sat at the kitchen table discussing possible names when Frank burst in and yelled, "Let's call him Barnum!" Though it had no family connection and suggested a showmanship that seemed out of place in Kansas, the name Barnum Brown stuck.

The first years of Barnum's life offered few chances to live up to his name. As soon as he could walk, he hauled water, milked cows, and helped his mother raise lettuce and onions in the garden outside the kitchen window—nothing, in short, that would suggest the extraordinary life that was to come. He later wrote in his unpublished autobiography, "In the late summer, I sometimes milked 20 cows, morning and night, sitting on a one-legged stool, so if a cow kicked I would fall over without resistance."

When Barnum grew old enough to work with his father, he loved following along behind the team of oxen as they stripped layers of soil off the land in William's never-ending search for new seams of coal. Sometimes as much as eighteen feet of dirt and rock needed to be removed before he found one, leaving makeshift mountain ranges of discarded rubble for Barnum to play on. When the boy wasn't climbing, he was digging, and he soon began to notice that some of the rocklike objects he found seemed like they belonged on a beach.

He began holding on to as many of them as he could find, with the help of his father, who "though untrained in geology, encouraged me in making these collections, for he thought that by doing so we could find out why seashells could be entombed in a Kansas hilltop 650 miles from the nearest seacoast today, the Gulf of Mexico," Barnum later wrote. Soon, he was storing so many specimens inside his room that his clothes could no longer fit in his drawers, leading his mother to banish his shells to a nearby shed. There, Barnum unintentionally followed in the footsteps of his namesake. "This became my first museum, where I had my first experience as a showman regaling visitors with these treasures, together with the Indian arrow points and scrapers I picked up while plowing our cornfields," he added.

The boy had somehow stumbled onto the most pressing question in science—how old was the Earth? In the late 1600s, James Usher, an Anglican archbishop, had seemed to settle the question by adding together the life-spans of every named descendant of Adam in the Bible and cross-referencing them with the Hebrew calendar. He concluded that God created the Earth on the night of October 23, exactly 4,004 years before the birth of Christ. This was considered a landmark feat of scholarship.

Miners were among the first to realize that the planet was much older than a literal interpretation of the Bible would suggest. When miners dug deeper and deeper into the Earth in search of vast mineral wealth, they kept coming back with things that shouldn't have been there if God had created the world in an orderly seven days some six thousand years ago, as the Bible suggested. Why were the bones of what appeared to be ancient fish uncovered far below the ground of open plains? Why were strange skeletons that didn't seem to match any living things found poking out of cliffs and marshes? And, if seashells found at the top of high mountains were evidence of the Great Flood, as some scholars believed, then why weren't the surrounding rocks smoothed by the erosion of such an immense amount of water? Rather than the neat process of Creation described in the Bible, Earth seemed to be covered with the scars of chaos.

In the mid-eighteenth century, a young German by the name of Abraham Werner enrolled at the prestigious Freiberg School of Mining. While most of his fellow students were learning where to find silver and how to match up the mineral formations they found with what they learned in the Bible, Werner noticed that Earth's crust seemed to be made up of four categories of rock that always appeared in the same order. He described the layers from the oldest and deepest to the newest and most shallow as follows:

- **Primary rocks, containing formations such as granite that contained no trace of life**
- **Transition rocks, including slate and graywacke and the first appearance of fossils**
- **Secondary layer, made up of sandstone and gypsum and other rock formations that were bursting with evidence of long-dead plants and animals**
- **Tertiary layer, consisting of sand and clay and an abundance of subterranean life-forms that could be found just by digging in the ground with your bare hands**

In Werner's time, fossils were widely recognized as something more than strange stones, though what exactly they were remained unclear. Aristotle was among the first to theorize that some material that appeared to be rock was once animated with life. This idea was not universally accepted, however. Centuries later some European religious thinkers proposed that perhaps the stones taking the form of bizarre animals or plants were God's way of ornamenting the interior of the Earth, much like flowers decorate its surface. Or perhaps they were placed there by God as tests of faith.

In any case, the fossilized relics of life—bones, shells, teeth, or leaves—are not in the strictest sense the biological remains of what was once a plant or animal. Instead, they are inorganic minerals like calcium that linger after tissues and blood cells have decayed, essentially becoming rocks that are in the exact shape of the original living material. Werner was concerned not with the history of life on Earth but only the composition of the planet that sustained it. After studying those repeated, stratified layers of material beneath our feet, Werner concluded that the entire planet had once been a vast ocean from which Earth's crust slowly emerged over more than a million years.

In Scotland, a farmer and naturalist by the name of James Hutton agreed with Werner that Earth had a history longer than anyone thought. So much longer, in fact, that he would later write "that we find no vestige of a beginning and no prospect of an end." But Hutton had his own theory that the planet's surface was part of a continuous cycle he called the great geological cycle:

- **sediments on land are carried to the ocean**
- **they are compacted into bedrock on the seafloor over time**
- **the sediments are ejected back above the surface by volcanoes and other eruptions from deep within the earth**
- **the process begins again**

The cycle he described meant that what appeared to our eyes as unmovable mountains had once been rocks buried on the bottom of the ocean, with the changes ticking along at a scale of destruction slower and more momentous than we can imagine.

As evidence, he pointed to a peninsula on the east coast of Scotland where horizontal layers of red sandstone mix with a string of vertical layers of gray shale, a disorganized arrangement far different from Werner's idea that all types of stone are found in uniform layers. What Hutton observed could only be explained by the violent churn of the planet weaving bands of rock formed on land with those formed undersea over millions of years.

Geology, it seemed, was anything but the neat-and-tidy study of rocks. Instead, it was a window into an abyss of time so deep that it was nearly impossible to understand. Was Earth a million years old? A billion? More? And if the planet was so old and the record of human life in the Bible dated back only six thousand years, what if anything took place during those missing millennia? Recognizing a threat to their explanation of the world, religious scholars downplayed both the significance and relevance of the dangerous new science.

For all of the existential questions it raised about life on Earth, geology was too valuable to ignore. Hidden inside the Earth were minerals, precious metals, and soon-to-be-important oil fields that were worth a lot of money. Treasure hunters cared little about geology's cosmic significance as long as this new branch of science could help them get rich. In 1859, for the first time, the financial value of manufactured industrial products built in the country exceeded the value of everything grown or produced on its farms. The search for the raw materials that the new economy relied on quickly became a booming industry.

As Barnum Brown grew older, iron machines began to replace oxen in the fields; telegraphs stood in the place of handwritten requests for another shipment of coal. The pace of change seemed to sweep him up along with it, instilling in him a sense of restlessness that could never be fulfilled on a farm. Excitement seemed to emanate off him and enchant everyone he met. As a teenager, he was tall, lean, curious, and fully aware that his twinkling blue eyes made him handsome. Carbondale could simply not keep up with him. There wasn't even a high school to keep his mind distracted from wondering what life was like at the far ends of the train tracks.

Barnum's parents knew that any energy spent trying to tether him to the farm was wasted. In 1889, they made plans for him to move to the university town of Lawrence thirty-five miles away, where he could attend high school before enrolling in the University of Kansas. Before the sixteen-year-old left home, however, his father took him on one last adventure to see the world together while they could. "Father wanted me to see what was left of the Old West before it faded away, to show me some of the places he had been in his pioneer days, and to broaden the outlook of an adolescent farm boy who had never been more than twenty miles from home," Barnum wrote.

Together, they packed a covered wagon with enough sugar, bacon, flour, beans, raisins, and coffee to last them four months on the plains. They headed north, waking up each morning before sunrise so that Barnum could prepare them breakfast while his father fed the team of horses, and stopping in the afternoon when they found good grazing land. They would repeat the same process at night, with his father taking the extra step of padlocking the animals to the wagon. He was worried that the smell of Barnum's cooking would bring unwanted attention as they passed through the quilt of lands belonging to the Comanche, Kiowa, Sioux, and other tribes who still roamed the Plains in diminished numbers.

As they rode, William told his son tales of a world that no longer existed. Bison were once so plentiful that his father had witnessed "great herds . . . streaming across the Missouri River in such numbers as to stop the river boats," Barnum later wrote. The introduction of barbed wire, railroads, and bloodthirsty settlers carrying powerful rifles had exterminated millions of bison in the brief span of Barnum's life. He reported that "we saw only their heads, preserved by the long shaggy hair and tough hide, strewn across the prairies like small barrels."

In southeastern Montana, the Browns neared the site of the Battle of the Little Bighorn, where thousands of Cheyenne and Sioux warriors had decimated Gen. George Armstrong Custer's force of 250 calvary some thirteen years earlier. The Browns then continued westward across the wide-open land, through what would eventually become Yellowstone National Park.

Only after they spotted the snowcapped peaks of the Rockies did William decide that it was time to head back, leaving behind the open country of his youth and the company of his youngest son to return to a present where he felt he had no future. "There were more new sights and every day was a fascinating adventure," Barnum went on. "It took us a little more than four months from start to finish. What an experience! This was Father's finest gift to me."

In the days after his return, Barnum readied himself for the move to Lawrence. As he boxed up his childhood, he packed shells from his personal museum to take with him, intent on finding a professor who could explain why the relics he found underground did not match the world he saw in the present day. He did a round of chores on the farm for what he hoped was the last time. He was young, ambitious and, thanks to the journey into the wilderness with his father, had the self-confidence to survive in any situation. At the age of sixteen, he set out in search of a life that could contain him.

CHAPTER TWO

A WORLD BEFORE OURS

L awrence, Kansas, is located about two hundred miles east of the geographic center of the continental United States, and, perhaps due to this central location, has a long history of being in the middle of things. The town was settled on the urging of a congressman from Massachusetts named Eli Thayer after the passage of the Kansas–Nebraska Act in 1854. This act allowed states newly admitted to the Union to choose for themselves whether to allow slavery. "Let us settle Kansas with people who will make it free by their own voice and vote," Thayer argued. A party of New England abolitionists heeded Thayer's call and selected a spot in the rolling prairie between the Kansas and Wakarusa Rivers for a settlement they named Lawrence.

Vicious fighting between pro-slavery and abolitionist settlers began not long after the town had a name. Ultimately, Kansas was admitted to the Union as a free state in 1861, three months before the start of the Civil War. Two years later, more than four hundred Confederate guerrillas torched Lawrence. It was rebuilt in months, a flurry of activity that Richard Cordley, an abolitionist minister, called "a matter of conscience." In 1865, the University of Kansas was founded on a small hill overlooking Lawrence. In 1867, the first locomotive reached the city.

The University of Kansas filled its halls with the sort of students who were not found in the elite institutions of the East Coast. The first student body of the University of Kansas consisted of twenty-six women and twenty-nine men, making it one of the first public institutions in the country to admit women on an equal footing. And the university made it its mission to show that the brains of the children of farmers were just as powerful as those of the privileged. To do so, it hired professors who welcomed the chance to do things differently.

It was a place ideally suited for a young man in a hurry like Barnum Brown. He completed two years of high school in Lawrence, then entered the university as an engineering student in the fall of 1893. After years of isolation on the farm, the fact that he was now surrounded by peers was exciting. It would soon become clear that despite his intellect, Brown was distracted by the school's social life, and his grades suffered as a result.

Amid the parties and pranks, Brown found time to pursue the explanations that had eluded him as a boy. The University of Kansas was still new, and that sense of being at the beginning encouraged students to seek out those who could answer their questions. A box full of seashells Brown had found at his family's farm was a daily reminder of what had inspired him to stretch beyond the limits of home. Hoping to get an explanation for the existence of these shells, he sought out Samuel Williston, one of the university's experts on geology. Though he had yet to have him as a teacher, Brown made his way to the office of the professor whom he would credit with changing his life.

Like Brown, Professor Samuel Wendell Williston was the son of migrants who came to Kansas in search of better opportunities. He grew up crammed in a one-room cabin with a family of six who never had enough to eat. Despite the hardships, Williston was naturally more bookish than his brothers, and at the age of fifteen he escaped to the Kansas State Agricultural College, where he began collecting fossils. After he graduated, Williston was hired as the primary assistant to Othniel Charles Marsh, one of the world's leading paleontologists, at Yale University. There, he had a front-row seat to a bitter feud that would become known as the Bone Wars, which greatly expanded the number of prehistoric creatures known to have once lived on Earth, but cost one man his fortune and another his reputation.

The term "dinosaur" dates to April 1842, when a wealthy professor named Richard Owen published a paper in which he argued that a new term was needed for the strange, enormous bones that were popping up throughout England. He combined the Greek word *deinos*—which means terrible or fearfully great, with *sauros*—which means lizard.

Owen's decision to label dinosaurs as a new order was inspired less by the light of new knowledge than by resentment of a less-connected rival. He grew up in the town of Lancaster as the wealthy son of a cloth merchant. With his father's help, Owen secured a position as an apprentice to a local surgeon and began treating prisoners at a county jail. He was soon called to assist in his first autopsy and grew fascinated with anatomy, seeing in the perfect architecture of muscle and bone the hand of God.

The focus on the anatomical structure of life led Owen to

consider the intent of its Creator. Were all species just as God had originally made them? Were the strong jaws and narrow vision of a carnivore a sign that it was designed to be a predator while the hooves and flat teeth of herbivores a sign that they were predestined to be prey? Or did life forms change over time? Already, science had abundant evidence in the form of folklore that the history of life on Earth was not a straight line.

Ancient discoveries of fossils likely served as the basis for legendary creatures such as dragons and sea serpents, as cultures around the world looked to explain the meaning of these bones of no-longer living creatures. Tattoos of griffins—mythical eagle-beaked lions with powerful wings—decorated the skin of nomads who lived five centuries before the common era and whose mummified remains were discovered in the Altai Mountains of Central Asia. But few scholars at the time would stoop to believing that stories of fancy could have a basis in fact, even though *Protoceratops*, beaked dinosaurs the size of sheep whose profiles look remarkably like those of griffins, were found throughout that same mountainous region.

A vase from the sixth century BCE shows Heracles rescuing Hesione from the Monster of Troy, and the monster's skull closely matches that of an extinct giraffe whose remains are widespread throughout Greece and Turkey. In North America, Algonquins recognized what they called "the bones found under the Earth" as ancient demons killed by the heroic god Manabozho, while the Blackfeet considered dinosaur fossils "the grandfathers of the buffalo."

In Asia, what we now call dinosaur fossils were once considered "dragons' bones" and often ground into fine powders for tonics and medicines, while artwork found in the Mokhali Cave in the southern African nation of Lesotho shows what appears to be a dinosaur leaving footprints across the valley. Over time, the abundant remnants of prehistoric life made it harder to believe that they were all the relics of monsters defeated by ancient heroes. The ease with which fossils were found in North America made it difficult to find supernatural explanations for something so commonplace.

A French baron named Jean-Léopold-Nicolas-Frédéric Cuvier, known to many as George, established the concept of extinction in a 1796 lecture that challenged the commonly held belief that all life fit into an unchanging Great Chain of Being that ended in God. After examining bones found in Siberia that included a three-and-a-half-foot-long femur and several teeth that weighed more than five pounds each, Cuvier argued that they matched up with no living animal. "What has become of these two enormous animals of which one no longer finds any living traces," Cuvier asked his audience, unveiling the bones of what we now know as a mammoth. They "seem to me to prove the existence of a world previous to ours, destroyed by some kind of catastrophe."

Though he recognized that some forms of life have disappeared from the Earth, Cuvier did not make the jump that the ones that remained could evolve based on their environment. And he argued fiercely that anatomy cannot take half-steps on the way toward a new species. In this, he agreed with religious scholars who thought that the concepts of extinction and evolution would inspire people to abandon all morality by lessening the value of human life.

Richard Owen was enrolled at the Royal College of Surgeons in London in 1827 when Cuvier traveled to London to view the Royal College's collection of fossilized fish. Owen was named his assistant because he was one of the few students who spoke fluent French. They struck up a friendship, with the young, gangly Owen becoming a constant companion of the portly, sixty-one-year-old Cuvier, whom people unflatteringly called the Mammoth behind his back. Interacting with a giant in the field only increased Owen's ambition to rise higher. Once, when he was introduced as the "Cuvier of England," he complained in a letter that "I wish they would be content to let me be the Owen of England."

The only problem was that others kept getting in his way. In 1811, a twelve-year-old girl named Mary Anning living in southwest England unearthed the complete skeleton of an unknown bug-eyed creature that looked to have the head of a crocodile, the beak of a bird, and the body of a giant, slender fish. Anning, whose father had died in debt and whose mother relied on charity to feed her children, sold the skeleton to a local lord for £23, enough to support the family for six months. The creature was soon taken to the British Museum, where English and French naturalists debated what exactly it was. Charles Koning, the Keeper of Natural History at the British Museum, named the animal *Ichthyosaurus*, meaning fish-lizard.

Curious naturalists began showing up at the Anning house and asking if Mary had anything new to sell them. She was often seen venturing below the cliffs wearing a long, dark dress, red scarf, and white bonnet, clutching a pickaxe in one hand and a basket to hold her finds in the other. Anning's specimens were the chief attraction in a small shop her family opened a few blocks from the shore. It was there that she interacted on a near-equal footing with some of the wealthiest men in the specialized realm of fossil discovery. This was a dizzying turnabout for a girl whom the local townsfolk had always found a bit odd even before she started pulling strange bones out of the ground—an opinion perhaps formed after she survived a lightning strike that killed three adults standing near her.

Anning had neither the wealth nor the status to formally study the fossils she found. This allowed others to claim the credit for her discoveries. She was paid small sums for each specimen she unearthed, while scholars and naturalists used her work to brighten their own careers. Among them was Owen, who attempted to flatter Anning by going on a prospecting trip with her. This was one of the very few times he set foot in a fossil dig in the field. Anning was guarded around him, and he left empty-handed. "She says the world has used her ill and she does not care for it," a friend wrote. "According to her account, these men of learning have sucked her brains, and made a great deal by publishing works, of which she furnished the contents, while she derived none of the advantages."

Anning was not the only one digging through England for fossils in hopes of securing a foothold in a better life. While she prospected in Lyme Regis in southwestern England, a shoemaker's son named Gideon Algernon Mantell could be found on the banks of the River Ouse approximately 150 miles to the east, sifting for what he called "medals of creation" that represented "the wreckage of former lives turned to stone." Mantell was a country doctor who had a preoccupation with the past. His now-lowly family could trace its lineage to a knight who had accompanied William the Conqueror in 1066 during the Norman conquest of England. In 1554, however, the family estates were seized by the Crown after Sir Walter Mantell was executed by Queen Mary, the monarch known as "Bloody Mary."

"In my boyish days I fancied I should restore its honors and that my children would have obtained the distinctions our knightly race once bore," Gideon Mantell wrote.

When he came across a newly opened quarry in the Weald region of southeast England, which exposed layers of sediment up to forty feet deep, he climbed down into it and began collecting fragments of teeth and shells. Mantell spent much of his free time chiseling through rock to unveil the fragments of what he soon identified as the femur and ribs of unknown animals. One section of a rib stretched twenty-one inches long; a thigh bone measured almost thirty. How much food would something so giant need to eat each day? How could a muscle ever be strong enough to move the bones of a creature that was larger than a house? If not for the fact that he was holding the fossils in his own hands, he would not have believed that creatures of this enormous size could have existed.

One morning in 1820 or 1821, Mantell brought along his wife, Mary, on his medical rounds. While he was with a patient, she passed the time by sorting through a pile of stones on the edge of the road. Among the items she picked up was a smooth object the color of mahogany that was more than an inch long and, upon closer inspection, looked to be a fossilized tooth. When Mantell returned, he immediately seized on the importance of her discovery. The tooth had a broad, flattened surface like those of mammalian herbivores, yet nothing in science at the time suggested that mammals had lived in the prehistoric era. The tooth was unlike any fish, turtle, or amphibian fossil, and seemed to imply something else entirely.

A tooth was not enough to prove the existence of an entirely new form of life, nor were fossilized fragments of bone. Yet together, they provided a wealth of evidence that was impossible to disregard. Mantell, forever looking for a chance to restore his family's past glory, grew convinced that he had discovered "one or more gigantic animals of the Lizard Tribe" that were altogether different from the type of fish-lizard uncovered by Anning. He began sending the bones and teeth he found to eminent geologists such as Cuvier.

In his letters, he argued that he had found evidence of what he called an *Iguanodon*, a name derived from the fact that the tooth Mary Mantell found resembled those of an iguana, yet was many times larger. When, in 1832, workers at a quarry in Tilgate Forest discovered fragments of petrified bone after blasting a particularly hard section of rock, Mantell bought the lot and had them carted to his home some thirty miles away. He spent weeks chiseling away until he could identify several vertebrae, ribs, and a sternum, along with more than ten strange bones that were seventeen inches long and had no apparent purpose. Only after trying to place them in different sections of the body did he realize that they were in fact a form of armor that ran down the spine. He called the creature *Hylaeosaurus*, meaning forest lizard, and with that identified the first of what are now known as a family of armored dinosaurs called ankylosaurs.

With *Iguanodon* and *Hylaeosaurus*, Mantell was responsible for the discovery of two of the three species of what we now call dinosaurs that were known to science at the time. (The other, a carnivore with serrated, bladelike teeth known as *Megalo-saurus*, was found by Rev. William Buckland at a slate quarry in Stonesfield.) Unable to shake the feeling that he might find a beast that measured over two hundred feet long, Mantell recentered his life around fossils, letting first his marriage and then his medical practice fail. As he rose up the social ladder, he received invitations to speak before the celebrated Geological Society in London, where he spoke with the sort of privileged men inclined to look down on country doctors.

Among them was Richard Owen, whose desire to put his own stamp on the biological record was heightened when the Geological Society proposed renaming Abraham Werner's layers of rock that had been classified by the type of stone with new names based on the life-forms found within each layer. In 1841, the layer that was once known as the primary rocks was rechristened the Azoic era, implying the absence of life. The layer of transition rocks was renamed the Paleozoic era, meaning ancient life, while the secondary rock layer became known as Mesozoic era, meaning middle life. The tertiary rock layer became known as the Cenozoic era, identifying it as the home of newer forms of life.

Owen realized that the pages of the history of life were waiting to be filled in, and he wanted to be the one who did it—or at least to receive the credit. Though he never found any fossils of importance, Owen began to criticize Mantell's interpretations of the anatomy of *Iguanodon* and *Hylaeosaurus* and the similarities between species. At times he implied that he was the first to identify anatomical features that Mantell had previously observed. Mantell considered such acts "piracy" and resolved to no longer share his work with Owen.

In October 1841, Mantell was riding in a carriage across Clapham Common in London when the driver lost control of the horses. Mantell fell while trying to grab the tangled reins and was dragged along the ground, severely damaging his spine. Over the following days, Mantell felt a sensation of numbness spreading through his legs and soon found that he was unable to walk. His work searching quarries and chiseling away stone appeared to be over.

Owen, meanwhile, continued to focus on the anatomical structures of Mantell's discoveries, and realized that the shaft of the *Iguanodon* femur was at a right angle to the pelvis, much like that of a mammal. This meant that it walked with its legs below it, like an elephant or deer, rather than with its legs splayed to the side, like a crocodile. Owen theorized that this also meant that it had a different center of balance than previously believed. Taking this line of thought further, this meant that the creature's tail— which had proven difficult to find in the fossil record and thus left him doubtful of Mantell's estimations—would be drastically shorter, reducing the *Iguanodon*'s overall length to well under two hundred feet.

In late 1841, a wealthy wine merchant and amateur geologist named William Saull purchased the first known sacrum, or lower spine, of an *Iguanodon* and installed it in his private museum. With Mantell unable to travel, Owen was one of the first to view it, and soon grasped its importance: the vertebrae of the lower spine were fused, just like the spine of *Megalosaurus*. That small adaptation allowed a creature's backbone to become incredibly strong, making it capable of supporting a body made of gigantic bones and mammoth muscles. A fused spine was not found on *Ichthyosaurus*, nor on any of the other apparent sea creatures that Mary Anning had discovered, suggesting to Owen that there had once been a distinct group of enormous reptiles that, like contemporary mammals, were designed to walk upright on land with their legs tucked under them.

Though he excluded other prehistoric reptiles that would eventually become recognized as belonging to the same group,

Owen focused on the similar anatomical characteristics of *Iguanodon, Hylaeosaurus,* and *Megalosaurus,* and argued they were large, unintelligent beasts that walked on all fours—sort of reptilian rhinoceroses. Over the next several weeks, he played around with different names for them, before settling on the term "dinosaur," which he introduced in an 1842 speech. With that, he claimed for himself the work that Mantell had done over the past twenty years, and within months attained the glory that would forever elude his rivals. The prime minister commissioned an oil portrait of Owen to hang in his home, and followed it up with a letter to the queen recommending that Owen receive a royal pension equivalent to $20,000 a year in today's dollars.

Mantell seethed in a letter to a friend that Owen had "altered names which I had imposed, and stated many inferences as if originating from himself when I had long since published the same," but had little recourse. His health continued to deteriorate, leaving him with few distractions beyond fueling his loathing of Owen. "It is astonishing with what intense hatred Owen is regarded by most of his contemporaries, with Mantell as arch-hater," said Thomas Henry Huxley, a prominent backer of Darwin at the time and whose grandson Aldous would go on to write the novel *Brave New World.*

The study of dinosaurs remained largely confined to England for the next thirty years until Arthur Lakes, an Oxford graduate, immigrated to the United States and later settled in Colorado to work as a schoolteacher. While on a walk with his friend Henry Beckwith in the spring of 1877, Lakes uncovered bones the size of tree trunks. With a few minutes of searching, they uncovered a vertebra nearly three feet in circumference that required the strength of three men to lift it into a cart. "It was so utterly beyond anything I had ever read or conceived possible that I could hardly believe my eyes," Lakes would later write.

He sent a few samples of the fossils to Othniel Charles Marsh, a professor at Yale University, who was the famed first professor of paleontology in the United States. As a solitary child who had often clashed with his father after his mother's death from cholera, Marsh spent much of his time alone exploring minerals exposed by the digging of the nearby Erie Canal. After he graduated from Yale, Marsh led some of the first paleontology expeditions in the United States through what would become South Dakota, Nebraska, Utah, and Wyoming. Marsh's position at Yale was paid for by his uncle, George Peabody, who had built a fortune through setting up a transatlantic trade in commodities and a banking firm in London. Peabody's success made him one of the richest men in the United States, and his attempts to give most of his wealth away made him one of the most famous.

The gulf in personality between uncle and nephew could not have been wider. At his death, Peabody was praised for a principled life marked by "charity and good will toward mankind." Marsh, on the other hand, seemed cold and suspicious. Had it not been for his uncle's support of Yale's Peabody Museum and his position as its director, Marsh would have been too disliked to rise higher.

The few friends Marsh had did not stay friends for long. Among them was Edward Drinker Cope, a onetime professor of zoology at Haverford University in Pennsylvania. The two men both searched the continent for the sort of prehistoric bones unearthed in Europe, but the similarities did not end there. Like

Marsh, Cope had found the study of the natural world a refuge as a child, and later admitted that he was "not constructed for getting along comfortably with the general run of people." He could not meet the harsh standards of personal conduct at Westtown, an elite Quaker boarding school, and often earned demerits for talking too much or poor penmanship. He dropped out of school in frustration and shunned his father's offer to buy him a farm, and instead pursued a scientific career without a formal university education. Throughout his life, he never lost the rough sheen which was at odds with his privileged upbringing.

The pairing of Marsh, whose lowly childhood put him forever on the alert for an insult, and Cope, a man whose anger over his youthful failures always left him needing to prove his worth, seemed destined to end in ruin. The first sign that their paths would clash came not long after Cope, who had quit his position at Haverford, alerted Marsh to fossils uncovered in Haddonfield, New Jersey, by diggers searching for the rich mudstone that was prized as fertilizer. At the time, just eighteen dinosaur species were known to have existed in North America, and most of those were identified only by an isolated tooth or vertebra—nothing like the nearly complete skeletons uncovered by Anning and Mantell. Cope invited Marsh to accompany him on a tour of the mudstone pits in the spring of 1868. There, Cope introduced Marsh to Alfred Voorhees, a local miner Cope paid for small bones he uncovered while digging. In the months after his tour with Marsh, however, Cope received no discoveries from Voorhees and when he asked the miner why, Voorhees seemed evasive. Around the same time, Marsh announced the discovery and acquisition of new fossils without revealing their source. Cope suspected that Marsh had gone behind his back and paid Voorhees to send the best bones to him at Yale, though he had no proof.

The growing mistrust between the two men turned darker the following year. Cope came into possession of more than a hundred bones discovered by an army surgeon in Kansas, and attempted to piece them together. The animal appeared to be the first known example of a marine reptile with an oddly flexible neck, the initial member of an order that Cope proposed calling *Streptosauria*, meaning "twisted reptiles." Cope, who was twenty-nine at the time, prepared to present his findings at a major conference that summer and fully expected it to make his reputation. Despite his suspicions about Marsh, Cope gave him an early look at his interpretation of the skeleton, seeking respect and recognition from a man nine years his senior.

Instead, Marsh seemed to delight in pointing out all of the mistakes Cope made, starting with the most embarrassing: Cope had put the head where the tail should be. There was no such thing as a twisted reptile. Cope didn't believe Marsh, until he discovered the mortifying fact that the skull fit perfectly into the last vertebra of what he had thought was the rear of the animal. Ashamed and angry, he tried to destroy all copies of the flawed essay he had thought would make him famous. In its place, he found comfort in the idea of humiliating Marsh as revenge.

For the next twenty years, each man attempted to find more fossils, name more species, and write more papers than the other—a feud that would later become known as the Bone Wars. Arthur Lakes's discovery of enormous fossil specimens expanded the battlefield from the marshes of the East Coast into the canyons and cliffs carving the western half of the country. This land was newly accessible through the construction of the Transcontinental Railroad. There, everything seemed greater: fossils suggesting dinosaurs so big that they stretched imagination; the starkness of the landscape; and the prize of finding what very well could be the largest animal that ever walked on Earth.

In an untamed land, Marsh and Cope each raced to find as many bones as they could while trying to block the other from succeeding. They paid off informants, spread lies about the other, and publicly wished the other were dead. Marsh, with his abundant wealth and resources, often had the upper hand, directing teams of Yale students to open numerous quarries each summer and move on quickly if they did not immediately find something worthwhile. He also made an agreement with Red Cloud, an influential chief of the Oglala Lakota tribe, to lobby Congress for protection of Native American lands and self-rule in exchange for the exclusive right to prospect on tribal lands in an area of what is now Montana and Wyoming. Even with the playing field tilted his way, Marsh was not above playing dirty. On one of the rare occasions when he found himself prospecting near Cope, Marsh snuck into his rival's digging site at night and scattered unrelated fossils in hopes of confusing him.

The pettiness touched nearly everyone connected with both Marsh and Cope. Their assistants took on the conflict as their own. At a rural outpost in Wyoming known for its abundant fossil beds, prospectors working for Marsh sent spies into a camp of men working for Cope. In return, Cope's team locked their rivals out of a train station to prevent them from sending their haul back to Marsh on the East Coast. Before long, the opposing camps were throwing rocks at each other, as if all of Wyoming were nothing more than a sandbox.

Cope, consumed by his need to best Marsh, made up for his dwindling financial resources by publishing more than 1,400 scientific papers on topics ranging from dinosaurs to early mammals. Soon, his collection of fossils was the only thing of worth he owned, his inheritance destroyed by a consuming desire to beat the one person who fully understood his need to find and discover new species. His obsession with proving his superiority prompted Cope to donate his brain to science after he died and he challenged Marsh to do the same, convinced that whoever's brain weighed more would be proven the true intellectual superior.

News of their discoveries appeared regularly in the largest newspapers on the East Coast. Between them, Marsh and Cope discovered and named more than 120 new species, including some of the most familiar dinosaurs we know now, such as the bony-plated *Stegosaurus*, the long-necked *Apatosaurus* (a name meaning "deceptive lizard" for the way some of its bones resembled an unrelated aquatic reptile), and its closely related cousin *Brontosaurus*, meaning "thunder lizard."

Because of the well-publicized rivalry, farmers began to realize that scientists would pay a lot of money for the fossils they often uncovered while clearing land. This provided an incentive to keep and protect what were previously considered novelties at best and nuisances at worst. Men throughout the west who were brave enough to explore unforgiving regions also became fossil hunters—a new profession that had materialized out of the Bone Wars.

To compete with Cope, Marsh began putting his name on papers written by his assistants, ruining what little loyalty they felt toward him. Samuel Williston, who would one day become

Barnum Brown's professor at Kansas, was among those who found their careers blocked by Marsh's habit of taking credit for others' work. He wrote a private letter to Cope complaining that Marsh "has never been known to tell the truth when a falsehood would serve the purpose as well." Cope shared the letter with a newspaper reporter in an attempt to publicly discredit Marsh. This betrayal severed Williston's ties with Marsh, forcing him to leave Yale. Williston returned to Kansas as a professor in 1890.

Marsh's status had been so damaged by the scandal of his behavior toward Cope that his funding from the U.S. government suddenly became scarce, and he retreated further into the sanctuary of the Peabody Museum. There he remained unrepentant and fearful that someone would one day find dinosaurs that made his achievements look small by comparison. Through their feuding, Cope and Marsh had effectively sabotaged themselves, clearing the stage for the start of another era, like a new layer of sediment laid down on top of their discoveries.

Free of Marsh's shadow, Williston finally had the time and money to launch his own expedition, blessed in part with a location in Kansas that kept costs lower due to its proximity to great fossil beds filled with the unknown. He had seen some of the great fossils lying scattered in the west, and knew that others were just waiting to be found. All he needed were some students to supply muscle.

CHAPTER THREE

SCRAPING THE SURFACE

Throughout his life, there seemed to be no task that could discourage Barnum Brown. He appeared to pay no attention to hierarchy or rank. If he was interested in something, he would go for it, not stopping to think of all the reasons why he shouldn't. When he heard that Samuel Williston was planning an expedition to the White River Badlands in South Dakota in the summer of 1894, he talked his way onto the nine-person crew despite never having taken a paleontology class. He was twenty years old and wanted nothing more than to continue what he felt would be a life of ever-increasing fun, free to pursue his interests wherever they pulled him.

The party left Lawrence on June 13, 1894, reaching the Badlands nine days later after taking a boat up the Missouri River. Using the skills he learned on his trip through the west with his father, Brown cooked the expedition's food, washed their clothes, and did all the other small jobs that were required to keep a pack of ten men alive as they searched for fossils under blistering skies, torrential thunderstorms, and hail. In return, he learned how to turn his raw energy into skill.

Paleontology was barely fifty years old and still to a startling degree reliant on luck. Some fossils were discovered by hikers who just came upon gigantic bones sticking out of the ground or cowboys who noticed what looked like strange bison skulls sticking out of the ground while driving cattle through canyons. Most of the fossils that inspired Owen to invent the term "dinosaur" had been found by accident by miners and road builders and were given scientific value only when they fell into the hands of someone who recognized what they were. With the exception of Mary Anning, who could afford to prospect only close to her home, few paleontologists had the skills to discover new fossil beds themselves. Marsh and Cope could identify bones when they were brought out of the ground, but they remained dependent on those who dug into the earth for some other purpose and came up with the unexpected, like fishermen reeling in a shoe when they were trying to catch trout. In fact, the betrayal of paying off the other's sources of bones was what truly fueled their twenty-year-long Bone War.

Going into the field specifically to search for fossils was still a novelty. Paleontology required both physical strength and intellectual skill, and those who could combine both would soar to the profession's greatest heights. On those dusty, hot days in the Badlands, Brown received his first lessons in how to dig with purpose, learning to use mining tools to break apart the earth without destroying the treasures hidden within. It was a welcome respite from the classroom for a student just then realizing his academic limitations. Here, knowledge was the product of hours spent stooped over in the sun muscling closer to a potential specimen only to find that there was still more work to do, like opening a series of Russian nesting dolls.

Pickaxes and shovels were suitable for taking apart big rocks.

Rock hammers were the most useful when working near a bone. Digging knives and trowels were required when you were close enough to extract it. Anything more delicate than that required a pocketknife. Paintbrushes kept an area clean, and plaster would stop a newly excavated bone from crumbling once exposed to air. Dynamite was handy to clear an area—but use too much and you'd blow up what had sat untouched for millions of years. If blasting was impossible, then a scraper plow attached to a team of horses could take off a layer of twenty feet of rock and dirt. And there was nothing wrong with keeping the fossil encased in rock once you found it. That's what the hammers and chisels back in the campus laboratory were for.

Once Brown learned the fundamentals of *how* to dig, he needed to learn the art of *where* to dig. Honing the talent to tell fossil from stone is like acquiring a new sense, even for prospectors today. In these harsh environments, the bleaching of the sun can make it impossible to rely on color or weight alone. A conical shape may hint that the object in question is a tooth, while a curve or an unusually straight line may be the first sign of a bone. If it is still a mystery whether you are holding a rock or a fossil in your hand, there is one last resort: licking it. The tip of the tongue briefly sticks to fossils, yet will not stick to stone.

The confirmation that an object is indeed a fossil simply leads to more questions. A prospector often has to guess which way the skeleton continues on beneath the shell of rock and dirt. Sometimes, what seems like the logical path of a bone ends in nothing, requiring you to retrace your path to discover the point where it jutted off, if it did at all. Other times the bones seem to plummet deeper into the earth, forcing a guess about whether launching a further assault is worth it. And worse, what looks like the promising start of a femur or mandible will sometimes turn out to be nothing but the indistinguishable nib of a toe—a disappointment made worse by the days of punishing labor it took to confirm this. As a whole, the work of finding fossils amounts to a few moments of joy surrounded by days of toil.

The harder question is where to start digging in the first place. Finding a fossil requires the ability to see, outside the bounds of time, two different scenes at once: the immediate landscape before you, and what it likely looked like millions of years ago. So many expeditions were simply a search for the Mesozoic-era sedimentary rocks that had the potential to hold dinosaur fossils. Actually finding a specimen on some of these scouting missions was considered an unexpected stroke of fortune.

Searching for fossils took expedition parties into some of the most difficult terrain on Earth. The snaking red-striped sandstone ravines of the Badlands, their ridges jutting out like the Earth's bones, were once lapped by ancient streams and lakes. Animals that died either in or near the water could become covered by mud and silt, starting the process of fossilization. Over millions of years, the weight and pressure of additional layers of sediment turned the remains of once-living creatures into stone, and in some cases lifted rock formations that were once at the bottom of vast inland seas or rivers into canyons and gullies.

A paleontologist on the hunt for a fossil first looks for a subtle variation of colors. This can be a sign that different types of sediment came together in an event such as a flood that could have buried the remains of an animal within it. After color, the next sign of a fossil is often texture. Some bones are marked by countless little holes, while others are smoother and shinier than rock alone.

Brown seemed to have a built-in sense of how an animal's body was positioned at the time it was buried and fossilized. With a glance he was often able to tell whether a rock was actually a bone, or whether a team member's find was worth the additional physical effort to uncover it further. This skill made him invaluable. It was as if he had a magical ability. Sometimes he would disappear into picked-over quarries and come out with fossils everyone else had missed, a feat that happened often enough that it seemed like he could see layers beneath the surface.

Brown's first find was the skull of an *Oreodont*, a piglike mammal that lived in abundant numbers on the Great Plains 5 million years ago. "The Dr. is well pleased with my skull. It is the greatest find so far," he boasted in his field journal. Williston soon began to rely on Brown not only for his strength—few others on the team could manage the job of moving delicate, heavy objects up and down the ravines without dropping them— but for his patience. Fully unearthing a fossil required digging around the specimen and covering it all with hardened flour paste. This formed a protective jacket around the fossil until all of the remaining rock could be carefully chiseled away in a laboratory. Over the course of a month and a half, the team found the remnants of a saber-toothed tiger and other prehistoric mammals, but failed to find the bones of a dinosaur.

The following summer, Williston again hired Brown to work in the field on a trip to Wyoming in search of the skull of a *Triceratops*. The first known specimen of the species—whose three horns and parrotlike beak gave it one of the largest heads of any known land animal—had been found in the region six years earlier. A cowboy named Edmund Wilson saw what he thought was the head of a steer hiding behind some rocks on the bank of a gulch during a roundup and threw a lasso over it. Ranch hands who rode alongside him described it as having "horns as long as a hoe handle and eye holes as big as your hat." Upon closer inspection, Wilson realized it was the skull of a creature that looked like an alien. When he pulled the rope to try to drag the skull with him back to the ranch, it rolled to the bottom of the gulch, leaving just one of its horns intact. Word of the find soon reached Marsh in New Haven, and he sent an assistant curator by the name of John Bell Hatcher out to Wyoming with instructions to bring back the skull as soon as possible.

When it reached Yale, Marsh determined that the creature's head weighed half a ton. He did not know what to make of the creature, calling it a "strange reptile," and bestowing upon it the name *Ceratops horridus*. Other *Triceratops* specimens—which were also originally known by the competing name *Ceratops*—popped up over the next several years in the same region. The problem was not finding specimens; rather, it was getting one out of the field. The skull alone of one specimen discovered in North Dakota weighed more than three tons, requiring a team of horses to haul it out of a ravine and several broken-down carts to pull it across the prairie. No one had ever put a *Triceratops* on display, however, and Williston hoped that by finding one he could help build the small museum at the university while also giving himself the added pleasure of annoying Marsh.

Brown helped lead a team of horses north from Kansas, arriving near Lusk in the first week of July 1895, just in time for a wild Fourth of July. He was raised in a town where saloons were the only source of entertainment, and he was the rare person who felt comfortable in both the rough world of the frontier and among scientists who only ventured into the Badlands to excavate fossils they hoped to place in a museum. The open lands, the adventure, and the mixture of science and the frontier was his natural element, a place where he felt fully free.

Within two weeks of arriving in Wyoming, Brown helped find two *Triceratops* skulls—each one six feet long, four feet across, and three feet thick—embedded in a high sandstone bluff deep in the Badlands. Each specimen was among the finest ever recorded, a testament to Brown's ability to dig but not destroy. By the time the expedition returned to Kansas, they had collected an additional five tons of fossils, and Brown had built a strong enough relationship with Williston that the professor invited him to live in his house during the fall semester.

Williston soon received a letter from the American Museum of Natural History in New York, asking for a student who might be available to work the following summer as an assistant. Williston knew just the person for the job.

"Brown has been with me on two expeditions, and is the best man in the field that I ever had. He is energetic, has great powers of endurance, walking thirty miles a day without fatigue, is very methodical in all his habits, and thoroughly honest," Williston wrote in his reply.

Not long after Williston vouched for his protégé's abilities, a letter bearing a Manhattan postmark arrived for Brown. Inside it sat an invitation that changed the course of his life.

CHAPTER FOUR

CREATURES EQUALLY COLOSSAL AND EQUALLY STRANGE

S pending weeks in the wilderness searching for fossils was something Henry Fairfield Osborn had only dreamed about. For any other reason, the lives of a scion of Manhattan society and a man who had spent his childhood playing on mounds of coal would have remained forever distant, like opposite poles of the Earth. While Osborn's life was in many ways the opposite of Barnum Brown's, Williston united them to form one of the most important partnerships in the history of paleontology.

The eldest son of a founder of the Illinois Central Railroad, then one of the nation's most profitable and powerful companies, Osborn grew up in the gilded cocoon of New York City's aristocracy. When he was a year old, his uncle, John Pierpont Morgan, the most important man on Wall Street, would stoop down and play with him on the family's parlor rug. During the summer, he explored the family estate in the Hudson Valley, often swimming in the river with his family friend Theodore Roosevelt. The rest of the year he spent at the family's four-story brownstone mansion at 32 Park Avenue in Manhattan.

When his father was increasingly called away on business after the Civil War, the teenage Osborn began acting as the head of the family, controlling everything from the household expenses to travel arrangements for his siblings. When it was time for college, he went to Princeton because his maternal great-uncle, the Rev. Ebenezer Pemberton, had been one of its three founders before the American Revolution. Over time, Osborn began to believe that he was destined for great things, having never been exposed to anything that would give him doubts. The fact that he was not an especially brilliant student did nothing to dent his idea of himself.

Not that his grades would matter in any real sense. His path in life had already been cleared by his father, who expected that his son would join him in the railroad business after graduating. Free to explore without worrying about his future, Osborn took his first course in geology in his junior year, where he was first exposed to the revolution happening right under his feet. He became fascinated by the remnants of the Earth's history, seeing in the slow engines of geology and evolution a confirmation of his conception of God.

Marsh was one of the first to try to stand in the way of Osborn's desires, flicking off his presumptuous request as a college student to come to Yale to view some of the professor's fossils that had not yet been announced publicly. To retaliate, Osborn helped organize what would become known as Princeton's first Geological Expedition, in which eighteen students and two professors embarked on an eleven-week trip through Colorado, Wyoming, and Utah in the summer of 1877. The expedition went about as well as expected, given that it was made up of a group of young men whose idea of roughing it consisted of arguing with waiters in Europe.

The group did not find any fossils of note, but returned with their enthusiasm for the natural world undaunted. Osborn decided to build his life around science, ignoring his father's pleas to consider a more lucrative line of work. After two years of postgraduate work in New York and Princeton, he was named an assistant professor of natural history at Princeton in 1881. Like most of the things in his life to that point, Osborn's success would not have been possible without the connections and financial backing of his father, who agreed to pay his son's full salary, floating his son's ambitions on a cloud of family money.

Despite his advantages, Osborn did little to distinguish himself as a scientist. After several years of failure in the best laboratory on campus, built with donations from his father, he pivoted to vertebrate paleontology and proposed coauthoring a textbook on North American fossils with William Berryman Scott, his onetime companion on the Geological Expedition. Scott had built a reputation in the field while teaching all the paleontology courses at the university. Osborn knew little about the subject himself but, thanks to his ability to control the pipeline of funding, he expanded the paleontology department and cast himself in the role of supervisor. The position allowed him to take credit for his colleagues' work, which he would continue to do over the remainder of his career.

Osborn's father constantly reminded him that staying at Princeton was a wasted opportunity, given the power and prestige that could be forged in Manhattan. So in the late 1880s, Osborn began making his desire to move back to New York known to members of his father's social circle, and in 1890 he was offered a position heading a new department of biology at what is now known as Columbia University.

Osborn, however, had bigger aspirations than just trading one university position for another. He convinced Morris Jessup, a former railroad titan and friend of his father who was now the president of the fledgling American Museum of Natural History, to bring him in to lead the museum's new Department of Vertebrate Paleontology. Though it was a small department at an obscure institution, Osborn saw a way to bolster his own reputation by transforming the American Museum into a player in the rapidly expanding world of paleontology—perhaps the one branch of science in which Americans were more respected than their European counterparts. For that, he had to thank the man who had stood in his way—Marsh.

By positioning himself as the heir to Marsh and Cope without the weight of their scandal, the board of trustees soon voted to give Osborn what he needed to build the paleontology division. It was now his job to fill the museum's mass of empty rooms and capture the public's interest. For the first time in his life, Osborn would have an independent measure of his success or failure that could not be swayed by his father. To revolutionize the museum, he had to find a person he could trust to bring him the fossils and subsequent fame which he considered his due.

Despite the importance of dinosaur fossils to the growing under-standing of the history of life on Earth, very few people had actually seen one. Nevertheless, in the early 1850s, England's Prince Albert decided it was time to build the world's first life-size models of dinosaurs. He turned to Sir Richard Owen, and work soon began on an exhibit showing the prehistoric world that would serve as the centerpiece for the Crystal Palace, a

'There's no time to rest or celebrate but when you do reflect and remember, it's because **this group of players has something special**. I will try to convince them to carry on; in every training session it's about work. The most beautiful one is the Premier League – that is the most difficult and I think we have the numbers to win it in a normal year, but another team has done amazingly. But now we have to finish second and we have the cup and the second leg against Madrid . . .'

ON LIVERPOOL

'Today we showed in the most difficult stadium in the world the reasons we are champions – one of the proudest performances of my career. Unfortunately we lost, but congratulations to Jürgen and this fantastic team for the victory. It was a good game for both sides, for the Premier League; for the billions of people who watched this game, it was good advertising. How we react is the process we have to learn. I don't have regrets.'

'I said it was a goal. That's why he sent me off. It was the difference between going in at half-time 1-0 and 2-0. If you go in 2-0 at half-time, it's a little bit different. It's different when the first goal in Anfield is offside. **These kind of games, this competition – the impact is so big.** The goal for Gabriel Jesus in Anfield is a goal; it's not offside. It's a penalty from Robertson on Raheem Sterling right in front of the fourth official. Of course that has an influence.

'You'll have to ask Mike Riley and the big bosses about that. I'm not here to talk about the decisions over the referees or VAR. Don't ask me, ask them. I say, "Thank you so much" all the time. All the time I go to referees, I say, "Thank you so much".'

ON LOSING THE PREMIER LEAGUE IN 2019/20 . . .
'I am really sure that when Liverpool come to our house, we will receive them in an incredible way and they cannot complain. Of course we are going to do it because they deserve it.'

'I can imagine that when you have three-zero years without winning the Premier League and then you win the Champions League, you are focused. A team like us, who have won eight titles, **has passion for every single game**, every single competition . . . You are not going to win all the time. But when you arrive at the first title, maybe you think you have more chance.'

AND THEN BEATING THEM 4-0 . . .

'Every game is different, but I cannot deny that beating Liverpool, the way that we beat them . . . We beat the best team in the world right now and we know we can do it.'

ON CITY'S 4-1 WIN AT ANFIELD IN FEBRUARY 2021

'I have a lot of emotions . . . many things happening in the game. Gündogan missed a penalty – it's like a routine against them – but we started really, really well, doing what we want to do. In the second half, the way we reacted to the goal, the way we played with quality, made the difference. For many years we were not able to win here. Hopefully next time we can do it with people. Anfield is so intimidating.'

'The reason why City and Liverpool are always up there is because we try to play in this way. That's why the Premier League is the best.'

'Everyone in this country supports Liverpool, the media and everyone. Of course because Liverpool has an incredible history in European competition. Not in the Premier League, because they have won one in thirty years . . .'

'So I was wrong when I say everyone wants Liverpool in this country? Yeah? So United likes City more than Liverpool? Oh my God, I didn't know it. Is it true? Welcome if they want to join us in the street. **But they have to wear the blue shirt**.'

'My intention was never to change anything in this country. I'm very pleased how England has taken care of my family, myself.'

ON MANCHESTER
The weather! I have to take care of my skin . . .'

4. PEP ON . . .

WINNING

'If we lose, we will continue to be the best team in the world. If we win, **we will be eternal**.'

'It just isn't possible to always be at the top of the mountain. Bolt, Federer . . . we thought they would never stop winning, but it's not possible. It's just not possible.'

'I won twenty-one titles in seven years, three titles per year playing in this way. I'm sorry, guys. I'm not going to change.'

'The night after Madrid, we were calm. But when we landed back here, Madrid was absolutely gone in my mind. That is the only way clubs become stronger every year. To be in there again is good. **The mentality is the same – to be starving, hungry to win another one**. I learned in the big clubs I was at before about their history that when they win a trophy they go and take a shower and are thinking in that moment about the next one.'

'Since we won the Carabao Cup as our first title together, we have played eleven competitions. If we win on Sunday, we will have won eight. **Eight out of eleven at this level is incredible. There are no words to express my gratitude to these players.** It is honestly so difficult to do it and to maintain that. That is massive.'

'I think it's remarkable – the last nine titles, you win eight. So it's difficult for anyone to do it again, not just us but our opponents. I've won all six finals since I've been part of this group so I'm very satisfied. It's not just about winning one – **it's to show in every game that we try to win**. That's the best thing we can give for our club. We have a responsibility to win titles.'

ON WINNING A THIRD PREMIER LEAGUE TITLE IN FOUR YEARS IN 2021
'Every title, every Premier League is amazing. This is special because every one of us, we suffer for this pandemic situation.'

'In sport, only those who win stay in everybody's memory.'

'**Winning is the only thing that matters**, because it helps you survive a bit more.'

'I want to play to win and nobody can argue with my stats.'

'The best way of educating players is to make them see that they can win.'

'Victory gives you ten minutes of peace, **but then it makes you stupid**. In victory you have to realise what is not going right.'

BARCELONA

'It is said that it is easier to get a new wife than to change the club you support, and that is correct.'

'Barcelona is a place where winning the game is not enough. You are playing with the feelings of millions of people.'

TO BARCELONA PRESIDENT JOAN LAPORTA IN 2008, ON THE COACHING VACANCY
'You wouldn't have the balls to give it to me.'

AND BACK WHEN HIS COACHING CAREER STARTED
'I hadn't had any other offers. Nobody had phoned me. It is a privilege to be able to train Barça B.'

'I am no one as a coach. That's why I face this opportunity with such uncontrollable enthusiasm. **I've come here prepared to help in any way necessary**. I know the club and I hope to help these players and the idea of football that you all have to grow.'

AFTER HIS APPOINTMENT AS BARCELONA COACH
'I don't know if we will win, **but we will persist**. Fasten your seat belts – you're going to enjoy the ride.'

ON BEATING REAL MADRID 6-2 AWAY IN 2009
'It's one of the **happiest days of my life** and I know we have also made a lot of people happy.'

THEN 5-0 IN 2010

'What will prevail in history is not just the result, but the way we did it. It isn't easy to play well against such a strong team. We have to be proud. **It is a global victory** because we have done things differently and there is no other club in the world that trusts local people as much as we do.'

'Sometimes we felt scorned. Sometimes we were ashamed to celebrate titles. We have felt, for a while now, that we do things that are not being supported everywhere. So we have to do the work of an ant, of not responding to all the attacks.'

**ON WINNING ALL SIX TITLES ON OFFER IN
2009 (SPANISH LEAGUE, CUP, SUPERCUP;
CHAMPIONS LEAGUE, EUROPEAN SUPERCUP;
WORLD CLUB CHAMPIONSHIP)**

'The future is bleak, because surpassing
what has been achieved is impossible.'

TO THE FANS

'Life has given me this gift. You have no
idea of the love that I'll take home with me,
the feeling of happiness. I am just as lucky
as all of you. I hope you have enjoyed
watching them play.'

'I had the best years of my life at La Masía. It was a time focused on the most non-negotiable dream I have ever had: to play for Barça's first team.'

'Every year at Barça we'd achieve new ways to evolve from what we had already established.'

'I have grown up with the Barcelona method and I hope to stay true to it for the whole of my career. Why buy a striker for £50 million when there is one waiting in the youth team?'

'The style comes dictated by the history of this club and we will be faithful to it. When we have the ball, we can't lose it. When that happens, run and get it back. That is it, basically.'

ON THEIR CITY RIVALS

'There are teams that wait for you and teams that look for you – Espanyol look for you. I feel very close to their style of football.'

'My grandad was the nicest person in the world and had a huge heart. He had an enormous sense of compassion, so **he almost felt compelled to support the underdog**. In our village there was not a single Espanyol fan apart from him.'

ON LEAVING BARCELONA

'I would like you to understand that this is not an easy decision for me. Four years is an eternity as Barça coach. Four years is many years. I have given everything, and I have nothing left and need to recharge my batteries. **I have to recover**, and the only way I can do that is by distancing myself. Otherwise we would have ended up damaging each other.'

'What we have done has been exceptional because Barcelona coaches don't last long. I am leaving as a very happy man.'

'During my sabbatical, I told president Sandro Rosell that I would be going 6,000 kilometres away from him. All I asked was that he leave me in peace, but he has chosen not to do that. He has broken his promise. I did my time and then I left. Let them get on with their own business now. I wish them all the luck in the world because in some small way their success is my success. I don't need to tell you what that club means to me.'

ON WEARING A RIBBON FOR CATALUNYA
'If they want to suspend me – UEFA, Premier League, FIFA – it's OK. People are in prison. They are still there. So, until they are out . . .'

TACTICS

'Tactics are so important because everybody has to know what they have to do on the pitch. The relationships and behaviour off the pitch between team-mates have to be as good as possible.'

'Football is such an indecipherable and complicated game. When I started, I did not know much about football. I had talent, but could not see the bigger picture.'

'Ideas belong to everyone and **I have stolen as many as I could**.'

'The dimensions of the pitch are the same everywhere. We play eleven versus eleven. What unites the team most is the ball. And the ball is on fire, so pass it. And when you lose it, you should want it back. **Get it back, and then play fast**. Those that play the ball quickly are the ones that can play with the greatest simplicity. There are no secret tricks, no magic potions.'

'It is as simple as that. We pass it to each other as much as possible and we try to score. Attack as much as possible, win the ball, and pass it to someone who is wearing the same colour shirt.'

'It's the ball that has to do the running.'

AFTER BARCELONA BEAT REAL MADRID IN
THE CHAMPIONS LEAGUE SEMI-FINALS
'We decided to play without a proper striker for the way they defend. They press so high – we saw it with the centre-backs – and there was space outside. We had ten free days and in those days I watched the most amount of matches of Real Madrid and their defensive game was different. They are so aggressive through the middle and when that happens, you have to make the pitch wide. We wanted to give diagonals as much as possible.'

'I look at the opponents. That's why we changed – the space was to attack, but never since I've been a coach have I gone to defend. Maybe I provide too much information. **I have to know the opponents**, they press a lot. They did that in the Camp Nou and I thought they'd do it at home – they steal the balls and make passes. You see after conceding the goal, you have to protect.'

'The line to win or lose is so tight. I have made changes many times that didn't work and were a disaster and today it worked but it doesn't count. Still, people haven't learnt.'

'The players trust the technical team completely, because **we're usually absolutely correct** in our predictions.'

'When you play as many times against each other, it becomes like the basketball playoffs. You do one thing; they respond with another; you answer in another way.'

'If there isn't a sequence of fifteen previous passes, a good transition between attack and defence is impossible. Impossible.'

'We need intense, precise work. We are aiming at a very specific style of play and must work extremely hard to perfect every move.'

'All I want to do is to share my game philosophy with the players so that they can reduce risk to a minimum and achieve their potential.'

ON TIKI-TAKA
'The intention is not to move the ball, rather to move the opposition.'

'I hate Tiki-Taka. I always will. I want nothing more to do with Tiki-Taka. Tiki-Taka is a load of s**t, a made-up term. It means passing the ball for the sake of passing, with no real aim and no aggression – nothing, nothing. I will not allow my brilliant players to fall for all that rubbish.'

'You have to pass the ball with a clear intention, with the aim of making it into the opposition's goal.'

'Barça didn't do Tiki-Taka! It's completely made up! Don't believe a word of it! In all team sports, the secret is to overload one side of the pitch so that the opponent must tilt its own defence to cope. You overload on one side and draw them in so that they leave the other side weak. And when we've done all that, we attack and score from the other side. That's why you have to pass the ball, but only if you're doing it with a clear intention.'

'I need time, but as soon as possible, we are going to try **to create team spirit**. That is the most important thing. After that, you can create tactics, but we have to create **something special with ourselves**.'

'When people mention our titles, I have to say that we did it all in a way we feel close to, in a way that respected the game, never forgetting that it is a game, a spectacle.'

'The guessing, the preparing, the switches during games, guessing what formation they will play, how we can surprise them too . . . That is what makes everything enjoyable, what gives meaning to everything.'

'All I do is look at footage of our opponents and then try to work out how to **demolish them**.'

THE
CHAMPIONS
LEAGUE

**ON MANCHESTER CITY'S QUEST TO
BECOME CHAMPIONS OF EUROPE**

'We cannot deny the Champions League
. . . With all respect, it's like the Queen.
Especially for us. We've never been there
before. Hopefully the pressure can
not be too much for us.'

'Last year was an extraordinary one
for us but people say, "But you didn't
win the Champions League!". That is why
I will be judged, if we don't win it in
my final period here, that I will be a
failure here. I know that.'

**ON WINNING THE 1992 EUROPEAN CUP
WITH BARCELONA**

'Ciudadans de Catalunya! Ja teniu
la copa aqui!'

'That night at Wembley was unforgettable:
my greatest memory.'

**ON BARCELONA'S 2009 CHAMPIONS LEAGUE
FINAL AGAINST MANCHESTER UNITED**

'I don't know if we will beat United, but
what I do know is that no team has beaten
us either in possession of the ball or in
courage. We will try to instil in them the
fear of those who are permanently under
attack. Oh, and I believe it is going to rain . . .'

'We took risks, we played three up front. **Nothing ventured, nothing gained**.'

'We're going to do this for Abidal. He has made it here and we cannot let him down.'

'We prepared everything, every single bit. We played well; we were the better team. The United players said: "What they have done to us today, that has never happened before".'

ON THE 2011 SEMI-FINALS AGAINST REAL MADRID

'A team that has won nine European Cups can never be written off. We are going to be careful and recover both emotionally and mentally.'

'We'll go out with respect for our world, the world of football, which sometimes makes me a bit sick. It makes me sick to live in this world, but it is our world.'

'This has been one of the most beautiful nights I have ever lived. We feel that we have knocked out a superior team, a wealthier club, that can pay whatever release clauses they want to sign a player, a team with seven strikers that anybody would love to have in their squad . . .'

ON BAYERN MUNICH LOSING 4-0 AT HOME TO REAL MADRID IN THE 2014 SEMI-FINALS
'The biggest f**k-up of my life. I got it totally wrong.'

'We played badly when we had the ball. **That's my responsibility**. I made a mistake. It was a bit better in the first leg. But congratulations to Real Madrid. We have to carry on now. If you don't play well and you defend set pieces badly, that's just how it is. We are being punished. We are at the highest level in Europe; **such mistakes are punished right away**. Bayern are a big side. I will try to lift the players again. It is a fresh experience now – surely something will stick. But it is too early for a general analysis.'

'I wasn't able to win the Champions League. I'm sorry about that. But this club and these footballers **deserve to win** it.'

'I am incredibly excited to play against Madrid, the kings of the competition. We would love to play them here, of course, in our city, and feel close to our people. But we will go where UEFA decides. If that's Porto or somewhere else in Portugal, we will go there.'

ON LOSING TO LIVERPOOL IN THE QUARTER-FINALS IN 2018

'This type of decision makes a difference.'

ON LOSING TO TOTTENHAM HOTSPUR IN THE QUARTER-FINALS IN 2019

'It is cruel, but it is what it is and we have to accept it. I support VAR, but maybe from one angle Fernando Llorente's goal is handball, maybe from the referee's angle it is not. I am so proud of the players and the fans. I have never heard noise like that since I have been in Manchester. Today is tough and tomorrow will be tough too but the day after we will be ready.'

ON REACHING THE CHAMPIONS LEAGUE FINAL IN 2021

'My first words are for the players who didn't play. I know how tough it is. My second are for our owners, chairman, all the people from Abu Dhabi. Then the players who played before for us – Colin Bell, Mike Summerbee. Then the guys that helped to take the club to another level – Joe Hart, Pablo Zabaleta, Vincent Kompany, David Silva, Sergio, who is still here. Many players helped us to be at this stage, we want to share it with them. **Without them it would not possible**. Of course, we've invested money in the last decade since Sheikh Mansour took over the club, but it's not just about this. If you want to think it's just about money, it's okay. But there is a lot of incredible things behind the scenes, a lot of people working, supporting and a clear strategy to do it. **What we have done the last four years has been incredible**, in terms of the Premier Leagues, the Carabao Cups, every competition we've played. To reach the Champions League final is so difficult. It's the toughest one but we did it. We've had an incredible Champions League season and now, **we deserve to be there**. We are going to play the final.'

AND AFTER LOSING 1-0 TO CHELSEA
'The players have feelings and soul and you know it hurts when you cannot achieve. For them now it's a new, new challenge to try. These guys win three Premier Leagues in the last four years, and every year we have the feeling that we can do better. We reached the final of the Champions League, so yeah, it's a motor. But there are many other teams who want it too. It depends on how you arrive in that moment, with injuries, with the mood, the karma for the team – many, many different things. **Sport is always a new challenge**; the past is the past, it's experience. It doesn't mean we'll do well this season.'

**AFTER BEATING SPORTING LISBON
5-0 AWAY IN FEBRUARY 2022**

'The result is a dream – I'm incredibly happy – but the performance we can do better.'

'In the Champions League, always I overthink. I overthink a lot. Absolutely. That's why I've had good results. **I love to overthink and create stupid tactics**. Tonight I take inspiration and there will be incredible tactics tomorrow. We'll play with twelve.'

AFTER BEATING ATLÉTICO MADRID 1-0 IN APRIL 2022

'Yes, we trained today to sit back for 90 minutes and get a 0-0 . . . Never in my life have I thought about doing this! Except when there's five minutes left and we have to defend to keep the result . . .'

'When you go to the Bernabéu,
there is no option but to win.'

'We've had incredible compliments. We have an incredible history. What we feel together inside is that we will remember this period with great satisfaction. But sometimes, to be happy, we get the proof from outside, and that is stupid. What we want is proof from the outside that what we've done is right, and I agree with most of the people who said that we've not achieved in Europe, we've not won the Champions League, and maybe they are right. **To get the recognition of everyone in the world, we need to conquer Europe**. Is it going to happen? I don't know, but what we've done here makes me incredibly happy, and first of all, we had fun.'

'No words can help for what all of us feel. It is just a question of time. Sleep as well as possible and think of the next target.'

'People say that if this group of players don't win the Champions League, they will be failures. I completely disagree. We know how difficult everything is, but I accept it. We're close – they know it, we know it – but **what is important is we are going to try again next season**.'

'We are sad, of course, because **we were close, but not close enough**. Madrid deserve it. The players wanted to play the final, but for this club to compete against Real the way we did is a joy. I say congratulations to Liverpool and Madrid, they deserve it. Next season we try again and, if it doesn't work, we try again.'

8. PEP ON . . .

MANCHESTER CITY

'I am so happy and excited. It's a pleasure to work here. I enjoy working with our players every day and we will try to do our best together in the coming years. As a manager, you have to feel good to be with the players – and I feel good.'

'We don't have the history – of United, Liverpool, Chelsea, even Arsenal – but there are many, many good things in this club and I'm privileged.'

AFTER A TROPHYLESS FIRST SEASON IN 2016/17
'If I have no silverware, I will not be here for a long time. No silverware – it will not be a good season. I knew that in August. **Being a manager depends on results**. I know what my standard was in the past and I know what is on my shoulders. I have to handle that. But I know we will be judged on the titles we have won. **My period in Munich was judged like a disaster** because we were not able to win the Champions League. I won three leagues in a row, we won two cups from three, we arrived every time in the semi-finals and finals but it was a disaster. I have to handle that but what I can say is **try to play better, better, better** than the previous month. That's what I want to see for the next year – be better.'

'Unless they sack me – which can happen – I will not leave. Why should I? I love this club. I like to be here. This is my club and I will be here, no matter. That's not just because I have a contract; **we want to fight to the end for the people who support this club**. I trust the club 100%, what they have done and they have explained to me. This situation is not finished and we will wait, but until the resolution is not done you have to play and play and that is what is going to happen.'

'Three years ago is different to right now. I'm not the same guy I was when I arrived here, and the players are the same. They have their dreams and after the dreams are accomplished, it needs another thing.'

ON SERGIO AGÜE . . . RO!!!

'The most important moment for this club – more important than when it, hopefully, wins the Champions League – is when Sergio scored that goal against QPR. It is much better than four titles in one season or whatever. And he was the guy.'

'To make back-to-back titles . . . For a long time it didn't happen, and we did it, so that means we have the mentality. But in sport you have to live in the future. Never can you have one eye on what you have done. Never forget that we are an incredible club and organisation.'

ON VINCENT KOMPANY

'I tried to convince Vincent to stay one more year with us – a lot. In the last weeks, I said, "No, no, no, you are not going to leave me", but he left me. When these guys take the decision, it is taken.'

'After training City, I won't ever train United. It is like I would never train Madrid. Definitely not. If I didn't have any offers, I'd be in the Maldives. Maybe not the Maldives because it doesn't have any golf courses. But in a place like that where I could play golf.'

'We have to continue. If we are not able to, then we want to try next season. Sometimes you don't win, the others are better, and you lose. The normal thing is not winning all the leagues and trophies. Sometimes you lose. The important thing is to not give up.'

'They gave me everything, so I cannot betray them or do anything wrong to them. That would be not nice from my side. Together we took decisions to come here and to extend the contract two times and it will be the same now. It depends how they feel about me and how I feel myself in the club. I'm not a guy to think much about the future when I have still the contract I have. I'm not good enough to think far, far away about my future because **my future always depends on results.** I'm not concerned for any second.'

'I would need an hour to explain what we've done at City. All the people before had the same idea. Step by step, we try to win our games.'

ON TRYING TO SIGN HARRY KANE

'We tried but it was far away from being done because Tottenham was clear that it was not going to happen. And when it happens two, three, four times, it's over. I've never created a fire here. I know they do the best for me.'

'I said a few weeks ago that we needed a
lot of points. We knew that and now we
really know it. Since October we didn't
lose one Premier League game, that
shows how good we have done.
Now we must recover.'

'We are not the best team in the world.
The best team is Chelsea, who won the
Champions League. The important thing
is in three days we go to Norwich
and have to win the game.'

'We have to fight to win the league. If we want to win, we'll have to win an incredible amount of points against an incredible opponent. The margin to Liverpool is nothing.'

'We have to feel the pressure that every game we play, if we lose, we are not going to win. Hopefully Liverpool will lose against us, but apart from that, I don't think they will drop points. We won fourteen games in a row; now we have to win eight games. Otherwise, we will not be champions.'

'We couldn't expect different with this Liverpool – they are almost the perfect team. We didn't expect to win the title with three, four or five games to spare. We've both done an exceptional season. We won't look at anyone else – we'll just try and win our game. I'm pretty sure the Etihad Stadium will be full and they'll be supporting us.'

'When I arrived, people here said the Premier League is so difficult, it is the toughest. Just Sir Alex was able to win four in five years and you realise the magnitude . . .'

'**We are legends. We will be remembered**. This group of players are absolutely eternal in this club. When you win the Premier League in this country four times in five seasons, it is because these guys are so, so special. **Winning at home in front of our people is the best**. The moment we equalised, we had the feeling we had the chance to score the third. It was the best atmosphere I have ever lived since I am here. Tomorrow we can celebrate together in Manchester's streets with our cigars and beers. I will bring my cigars, don't worry. Congratulations to Liverpool – they have made us better and better each week. Now it is time to celebrate. **We are champions again**.'

9. PEP ON . . .

PLAYERS

'I am not dealing with footballers, I am dealing with people. They have fears and worry about failing and making fools of themselves in front of 80,000 people. I have to make them see that **without each other they are nothing**.'

'Every footballer in the world has dedicated himself to a life of football because they once kicked a ball and they loved it.'

'I don't like it when a player says, "I like freedom; I want to play for myself." Because the player has to understand he is part of a team with ten other players. If everyone wants to be a jazz musician, it will be chaos. They will not be a team, and nothing will be possible.'

'Out of everyone at Manchester United, I would pick out Scholes. He is the best midfielder of his generation. I would have loved to play alongside him.'

'I like the type of player who is comfortable on the ball and who will dominate the centre of the pitch.'

'I think players like me have become extinct because the game has become more tactical and physical. There is less time to think.'

'Put the good players in the midfield. Get the good players inside, hold on to the ball and be aggressive. This is definitely the line to follow.'

ON SERGIO AGÜERO

'I've never seen such a big star be
so humble and funny. He accepts my
decisions when it sometimes doesn't work
for him. I've worked with other stars who
believed they were bigger than Sergio,
when they weren't, and they were more
difficult to handle and to be with. It's not
easy to find a guy with his status, his
personality and what he's done in
his career with his humility. He is
a joy to work with.'

'To break this record of Thierry Henry means it's not just for a short period, it's many years. To be the foreign player with the most goals and hat-tricks speaks for itself. It was an honour to be here on the day he achieved the record. He's a legend. I said many times, he will die scoring goals.'

'The best is Messi. Messi is a No. 9, a No. 10, a No. 11, a No. 12, a No. 6, a No. 5, a No. 4, whatever. But the rest is Sergio.'

ON LIONEL MESSI

'Messi is unique. A one-off. We have to hope that he doesn't get bored, that the club can give him the players so that he can continue feeling comfortable, because when he is, he doesn't fail. When he doesn't play well, it is because something in his environment isn't working.'

'**It has been an honour** to be the coach of the best player I have ever seen and probably the best I will see.'

'If Leo smiles, everything is easier.'

'The best player in the world in Messi.
And he doesn't run. There is no better
Cruyff disciple than him.'

**'There is no defence that can stop Messi.
It is impossible.'**

'If you train badly, you play badly.
If you work like a beast in training,
you play the same way.'

'I will forgive if the players cannot get it right, but not if they do not try hard.'

'How do I convince a player who I don't love and don't pick to play that I love him?'

'People don't spend the day before they go to work locked up in a hotel. We just try to make things the same for them. If they don't rest, they're not looking after themselves, and that means they'll play worse and lose their jobs. I judge my players on the work they do, not on their private lives.'

**AFTER MANCHESTER CITY PLAYERS WERE
OUTED ON SOCIAL MEDIA**

'The video didn't show exactly what happened. They had dinner together and they were sober. But they will be fined because they didn't invite me!'

ON ANDRÉS INIESTA

'Iniesta doesn't dye his hair, he doesn't wear earrings and he hasn't got any tattoos. Maybe that makes him unattractive to the media, but he is the best.'

ON RAHEEM STERLING

'All the clubs have to know that when Real Madrid or Barcelona knock on the door, the other clubs must tremble – they will be in a little bit of trouble. That is normal and I understand completely. But I don't know if Madrid or Barcelona called his agent. I don't have any doubts about his commitment from the first day to the last day.'

ON RIYAD MAHREZ

'We struggled a lot in the last years to score penalties but now it is a guarantee. He has the personality to say: "Give me the ball, I am going to score", and he did.'

ON KEVIN DE BRUYNE
'Since we were together he has been incredible – his commitment, his mentality. He's a spectacular player.'

'Unstoppable, brilliant, awesome, outstanding, perfect.'

114

ON GABRIEL JESUS

'Gabriel has something unique in the world. He helps us be more aggressive and he's a fighter. What we have to do is adapt his qualities for the benefit of him and of the team.'

'If there is one person in the world who deserves days like this, it's him. I'm pretty sure there is not one person who is not happy for him. But Gabriel doesn't need to put in a performance like that and score four goals for me to know exactly what he can do.'

ON BERNARDO SILVA

'First, his mum and dad have to be so proud because he's a lovely person. He's so generous, whether he plays or doesn't . . . **He doesn't just play football, he understands the game.** He understands every action, like few in the world.'

ON PHIL FODEN

'Put in the superlatives yourselves, I'm running out. It's already been a while now that he has been outstanding. He's more than decisive in every way. That he's capable of doing everything that he does at his age is something impressive, that doesn't make any sense.'

'I think he can play in all five positions up front: winger both sides, striker and attacking midfielder in the pockets. All his actions are so so quick. Phil's rhythm is always high.'

'I don't know if any important club in Europe plays teenagers every week when the demand is to win titles. We have the tendency in all countries to say someone will be the new Wayne Rooney, George Best or David Beckham after two games. I am a fan of respecting a little bit the process with young guys. Time is needed to make them believe "this is difficult".'

'It's much easier to train youngsters than it is older players. You feel like you're really coaching. With older guys, you have to watch and review what you say, how you say it. With the kids, you just take them by the scruff of the neck and bring all the talent out. Like squeezing an orange.'

ON VETERAN PLAYERS
'Just be with them, like young actors have to be with old actors. Become wiser and know the values.'

10. PEP ON . . .
ITALY

**ON BARCELONA LOSING 4-0 TO AC MILAN
IN THE 1994 EUROPEAN CUP FINAL**

'We went out there convinced we were
the better team and they put four past us.
Their superiority was so great that I just
wanted the game to be over.'

**FOLLOWING A FAILED DRUGS TEST
WHILE PLAYING FOR BRESCIA**

'The Italian justice system cannot look
me in the eyes. I am innocent.'

'Do you think I need an illegal substance
to play against Piacenza?'

BEFORE THE 2010 CHAMPIONS LEAGUE SEMI-FINALS

'We aren't playing against Inter; we're playing against ourselves. We are going to see if we are capable of being ourselves in the most important, transcendental game of our lives. Inter Milan don't even exist.'

AND AFTER BARCELONA LOST TO JOSÉ MOURINHO'S SIDE

'Criticising him would be looking down on Inter and that is not fair.'

11. PEP ON . . .
MOTIVATION

'At the end our job is to convince the guys that is the best way to go – the course, the road. So that is what it is. So the tactics is important, the training, the facilities, but at the end it is what I have to do to convince you. Sometimes, with you, we're going to take a beer in the bar, maybe it's the best way to convince you . . .'

'In football, **the worst things are excuses**. Excuses mean you cannot grow or move forward.'

'For me, the most wonderful thing is planning what is going to happen in every game. I always try to give the players the security of knowing what they will encounter. This increases the possibility of doing things well.'

'Some of you play better when you're angry with me. So **if you hate me, hate me**, guys. It's no problem at all.'

'You have to have lots of charisma, a strong personality, a hunger, a faith in what you do and what you believe. Every day, convince someone to be convincing; every day, accumulate more and more people who think like you.'

'I'm going to defend you until the last day in our lives in the press conference. But here, **I'm going to tell you the truth**.'

'**I am the leader**. Follow me, and we will achieve. We have to start work quickly and intensively. Whoever wants to be with us from the start will be welcomed. The rest – we will win them over in the future.'

'Every single training session, every single game, you have to be there, ready. I know your quality is there. I know you are talented players. But to become the top, top team, you have to learn to play football with courage.'

129

'I have never had problems within the team. The most important thing is to have a good relationship and respect with each other. They are enemies because they fight for the same position, but **at the weekend, they become brothers**. We know each other well and have good harmony thanks to the captains.'

'Personality is what we've done in the last five years, every three days. The same character and personality that lost in Madrid in the last four games has scored nineteen goals.'

'Keep running. If you stop,
that's it – you're out.'

'Mistakes come when you relax, if
you lose focus when you pass the ball, or
receive it, or press for it. It's when
you think everything is done.'

'You look into your players' eyes and it's
a bit like looking at a lover. Either you see
passion and a willingness to be seduced,
or you watch as the passion ebbs away.
It's all in the eyes. It's all about seduction.'

12. PEP ON . . .

GERMANY

'Beer and party, lederhosen and women in their frocks – it's going to be great. I'm looking forward to experiencing these three weeks. You can trust me.'

'It would be presumptuous to say that Bayern is about to embark on a new era. **We have to take it step by step**. Expectations are very high, and it isn't going to be easy. I'm actually a little nervous.'

'It's a bit surprising to be able to walk
about the city and go into restaurants
without people coming up to talk to me.
The people here are extraordinary.
They treat you with real respect
and leave you in peace.'

'Right now **we are all hungry**. The players,
because they have a new coach and
concepts to learn; me, because I want
to win with a different set of players.
Let's see if we can do it.'

'I want them to be more Bayern than ever. **Let themselves go, run, liberate themselves**! Let them run.'

ON HIS KEY PLAYER

'Lahm is a scandal. He is super-intelligent, understands the game brilliantly, knows when to come inside or to stay wide. The guy is f**king exceptional.'

'Philipp is a machine. He gets the ball and does whatever he wants with it. He takes it wherever he wants it to go and always in the right direction. If we win anything this season it will be down to what I did with Lahm.'

'I love midfielders. I'd love to have thousands of them in my team. Thankfully, I have Lahm who, even though he may be the best full-back in the world, can play anywhere. He could be our striker if we asked him. In midfield he's just prodigious.'

'**This league is remarkable**. I've never seen anywhere to equal the Bundesliga for the number of teams who can hit you with so many effective, massively quick counter-attacks.'

'The stadiums are phenomenal and the **atmosphere is sensational**, despite the rivalries that exist . . .'

'Dortmund are unique. I've never seen anything like it. They are completely focussed for ninety minutes, waiting for you to mess up a pass so that they can set their sprinters on you. I must take some time to really study this and see if there is any way to stop them. They're just so good.'

'My advice for Sebastian Kehl is: if you have a 35-point deficit in the league, **it is better to shut up**.'

AFTER BEATING WERDER BREMEN 7-0 AWAY

This is the first time we've played a great match using my definition of positional play. I'd like to thank the players for what they have done. **It's an honour to be their coach**.'

'Ich liebe euch! Ich bin ein Münchener!'

ON LEAVING BAYERN MUNICH

'Usually what happens inside the dressing room remains inside the dressing room. Whoever has spoken has done it to hit me. But I'm not here next season anyway, so it's not my problem, but Bayern's.'

'I'm going with the understanding that I've done my duty.'

13. PEP ON . . .

LIFE

'**I strive to live with passion** and not to be desensitised to life. Things matter to me. You've got to live like that. Otherwise, what's the point? It's not possible to please everyone and there is no point in trying to be what other people think you should be. **For me, it's important to be who I am**, not just to be different, but to be as authentic as I can be.'

'Creating something new is the difficult part. To make it and build it and get everyone to follow? **Amazing**.'

'I have always made a point of observing and reflecting on the things I see.'

'**I have learned that when you're in the right, you should fight the world**.'

'There are no general theories that apply to everything. And anyone can be valid; what doesn't work is imposing something that doesn't work.'

'I have always thought that everything
starts from looking for what you really like.
Finding that is the essence of everything.'

'I like the same as everybody:
wine, reading, family.'

'I sleep like a baby this year.'

'If I'm not satisfied, I go home and don't be the manager of Man City. I go to another league – in the Maldives, the Maldives League – and play one game a week and I'm so comfortable under the coconuts.'

'That's the beauty of sport. **Sometimes you laugh, sometimes you cry**.'

'Do you think I was born knowing everything?'

'I am always starving. I cannot live for one year thinking how happy I am.'

'Perfection does not exist, but you have to look for it anyway.'

'It's been a long journey. I'm happy, proud, happy with the way people treated me, and I have made many friends. I cannot ask for more. I have had many years in the elite. **I did not come to make history but to make my own history**.'

ACKNOWLEDGEMENTS

Getting to know Pep Guardiola, virtually, through putting together this book, has been full of unexpected twists and turns, much as the denouement of the 2021/22 Premier League (and indeed Champions League) season provided further evidence of the incredible way football can take over our lives. If anything, Pep has opened up more than ever as the years go by, as his emotional response to his latest managerial triumph demonstrated.

Pep had previously stated that he would only talk to the media in press conferences, which has made collating his words of wisdom an easier task. The story is related in Guillem

Balagué's seminal book *Pep Guardiola: Another Way of Winning*, which is essential reading, along with Martí Perarnau's *Pep Confidential*. Thanks must go though to all the journalists across the world who continue to disseminate Pep Talk.

Thanks too to the winning team behind this book – Robin Harvie, Jonathan Harris and Isobel Mehta – and to Tony, Martin and the late Jeff, City fans who suffered through the years before Pep, for their inspiration.

Finally, to my grandfather Bill, a more erudite author than me. He would have liked Pep.

ABOUT THE AUTHOR

Giles Elliott is a writer and editor who has worked with some of the top names in sport in his career in publishing, print and broadcast journalism, and now combines book projects with leading the horticulture team at a garden centre in west London. He was given the name Gilezinho by his Brazilian wife. He is the author of *The Little Red Book of Klopp*.

planned amusement park, zoo, and ornamental gardens in a southeast London suburb. To make the idea a reality, Owen hired a sculptor named Benjamin Waterhouse Hawkins, a former assistant superintendent of the London World's Fair.

With nothing other than Owen's drawings and theories to go on, Hawkins cleared his workshop and began constructing the first life-size

Henry Fairfield Osborn in 1890, shortly before he joined the fledgling American Museum of Natural History.

forms of dinosaurs to appear on Earth in millions of years. He began by crafting small models out of clay, basing the way that each animal's limbs and muscles hung from its body on Owen's conception that dinosaurs were large, lumbering, dimwitted beasts that mainly lived in or near water for relief from the strain of moving their enormous bodies. Once each model met Owen's approval, Hawkins forged full sculptures out of brick, iron, and cement that weighed up to thirty tons. Sea lizards, *Iguanodons*, *Megalosaurus*, and pterodactyls began to take shape in his South London workshop, slowly bridging the abyss of time between the Paleozoic era and the Victorian Age. Each scaly creation was painted a shade of light green, making it appear to be the joining of a garden lizard with a particularly tall and fat hippopotamus.

To build up the public's interest in the new park, Hawkins invited twenty-one of London's leading scientists and newspaper editors to dine on an eight-course feast served inside the *Iguanodon* mold on New Year's Eve of 1853. Owen sat at the literal head of the table, greeting each person as he climbed up a small ladder to reach the belly of the beast. The party went long into the night, with speeches heralding Owen's achievements.

The coverage of Hawkins's publicity stunt thrust dinosaurs into the public consciousness, sparking one of the first social manias based in science. Hawkins was besieged with requests to tour his workshop before the official opening of the Crystal Palace, and started a lucrative business selling miniature casts of his models. Charles Dickens wrote letters to Owen begging him to write for his journal *Household Words*.

When Queen Victoria opened the Crystal Palace on June 10, 1854, forty thousand people lined up outside. Sir Richard Owen stood with the French emperor and the king of Portugal as the queen gave a speech in which she said she hoped "that this wonderful structure, and the treasures of art and knowledge which it contains, may long continue to elevate and instruct, as well as to delight and amuse, the minds of all classes of my people."

Hundreds of thousands of visitors toured the grounds of the Crystal Palace over the next decade. Those who did not make the trip themselves could hardly miss the posters and models of Hawkins's creations that were widely sold throughout the country, spurring the imaginations of writers including Jules Verne and Louis Figuier, whose work soon featured dinosaurs sparring with one another. The models made the existence of dinosaurs real in a way that drawings of fossils could not. They upended the current conception of the world, forcing people to question everything they had always believed.

The worldwide popularity of Hawkins's models led the commissioners of the new Central Park then under construction in New York City to hire him to create models for a planned Paleozoic Museum—an exhibit featuring dinosaurs discovered in the American West. These larger, heavier, and presumably fiercer dinosaurs than their European counterparts would be a fitting way to demonstrate the superiority of the New World. The planned museum would attract millions to the new park and enhance New York's reputation with its own wonders to display.

In the ten years since Hawkins built the Crystal Palace sculptures, scientists had realized that there were fundamental flaws in Owen's conception of how dinosaurs moved. Instead of the heavy, squat beasts, new discoveries of fossils revealed that they were probably more lithe and active, with some as likely to move on two feet as on all fours. Hawkins traveled to Philadelphia to seek help from Joseph Leidy, then the country's leading expert on prehistoric life. Leidy let Hawkins view the bipedal *Hadrosaurus foulkii* at the Philadelphia Academy of Natural Sciences, which was the most complete dinosaur skeleton known when it was discovered in 1858 in New Jersey. Hawkins made plaster casts of the thirty-foot-long herbivore's bones and, with Leidy's input, created a hybrid of sculpture and anatomy. The only thing missing was a skull, which he improvised by crafting the head of an *Iguanodon*.

After two months of work, the result was the world's first standing dinosaur skeleton that appeared in a lifelike pose. The specimen was put on display at the academy in November 1868. Though the museum was open only two days a week, more than one hundred thousand people—twice the annual attendance in any year of the institution's history—passed through its doors to gawk at the bones. Due to the "excessive number of visitors," the academy's trustees decided it was time to charge an admission fee for the first time, a not-so-subtle way to discourage the poor from coming into contact with science.

Hawkins returned to New York to complete the models for the Paleozoic Museum, but soon ran into a new problem. The city was run by corrupt politicians, headed by William "Boss" Tweed, who stopped funding the proposed Central Park museum in order to shuffle money to pet projects. When Hawkins complained publicly, a gang of vandals hired by Tweed broke into his studio in Central Park on the night of May 3, 1871, and smashed every mold and sculpture Hawkins had built over the prior three years. The rubble was dumped in a pit in the northern stretches of Central Park, and the idea of a Paleozoic Museum was buried with it.

The fate of dinosaurs in Manhattan would now fall to a struggling museum founded by a relatively unknown scientist named Albert Bickmore, a Harvard graduate. Bickmore's reasoning for building a museum dedicated to science in New York City was as practical as his vision was not. "Science does not appear to create wealth directly," he reasoned, so it "must depend on the interest which rich and generous men take in it. . . . New York is our city of the greatest wealth [and therefore] the best location for the future museum of natural history for our whole land."

Bickmore made his way through the city's aristocracy, pitching the idea of a museum as a way to further the glory of their hometown while preventing rival cities like Boston or Chicago from one day eclipsing it. He eventually convinced nearly twenty of the city's wealthiest men—a group including

J. P. Morgan, Theodore Roosevelt (the father of the future president), and A. T. Stewart, who founded the first department store in New York City and amassed a fortune that ranks among the ten largest in U.S. history—to pledge their financial support for a new museum of natural history, and to ask the Board of Commissioners of Central Park to place it on public grounds.

Its name was a reflection of Bickmore's ambition: the American Museum of Natural History. From its birth in 1869, it was meant to be an institution that would have no rival in the country. Yet Bickmore was not the first person to call something the American Museum. Still alive in the public's memory was what had once been the most popular museum in the country, until a freak fire at the end of the Civil War destroyed it just four years earlier. That American Museum had been nearly the exact opposite of the prestigious place of science that Bickmore hoped to build.

EMPTY ROOMS

The mermaid burned first.

A wooden club said to have been used to kill the colonial explorer Capt. James Cook in Hawaii fell next in the path of the flames, followed by a case containing live boa constrictors that had dined on fresh rabbits before an audience of schoolchildren earlier that morning. As the fire spread to the upper floors, someone—perhaps a firefighter, perhaps a visitor—smashed one of the glass sides of an immense water tank with an axe, sending thousands of gallons of seawater cascading down the stairwells and leaving two whales beached on the second floor of a building in Lower Manhattan. Wax figures of Napoleon and Cleopatra, letters signed by George Washington, screeching monkeys of all sizes—seemingly everything that could be conjured by the human imagination soon came tumbling out of the windows, landing in a crowd that had begun to gather on Ann Street.

The fire continued to grow, destroying a place that was considered an essential stop on any New York sightseeing tour. It was a place as famous for its lies as for its truths, a collection of humbugs and spectacles that mirrored the mind of its founder, a man whose genius lay in letting his customers in on the fact that they could not trust him. Phineas Taylor Barnum—P. T. for short—seemed to embody the uniquely American belief that a good story was more important than fact. This mindset was a gift of his grandfather, who hoodwinked young P. T., spinning stories about prime farmland he would one day inherit and become the wealthiest boy in their hometown of Bethel, Connecticut. When Barnum turned twelve, he discovered that the place of his dreams was a hornet-infested swamp. "I had been the laughing-stock of the family and neighborhood for years," Barnum later wrote in his autobiography. "My grandfather would go farther, wait longer, work harder and contrive deeper, to carry out a practical joke. . . . I am almost sorry to say I am his counterpart," he wrote.

He carried out his first known swindle while working as a clerk at a general store near Bethel, selling thousands of tickets at fifty cents each for what he claimed was a "magnificent lottery." Its winners soon discovered that their prizes were empty bottles and other pieces of junk that Barnum had pulled from the store's unsold inventory. In search of new gimmicks, he tried opening his own store, ran a few more lotteries and briefly served time in jail after founding a newspaper whose specialty seemed to be losing libel suits. He found the success he was looking for in the creation of the American Museum, which opened in Lower Manhattan in the early 1840s.

He was not the first person to open a museum and fill it with the strangest things he could find. He just did it better than anyone else. The first popular museum in the United States was founded by a Philadelphia painter named Charles Willson Peale, who collected and displayed items ranging from a mastodon bone to Benjamin Franklin's taxidermized angora cat. Known as "cabinets of curiosities," these early museums were often little more than a collection of unique and strange things gathered during a wealthy person's lifetime, without organization or serious analysis.

After Charles retired, his son Rubens expanded these diversions to include magicians, funhouse mirrors, and biological "freaks of nature." Within a year, he doubled the museum's revenue and began casting an eye out for ways to expand. He opened Peale's New York Museum in 1825 and offered discounts to schools and students. On its four floors, exhibits ranged from colorful gemstones to a calf with two heads to a dog named Romeo who barked answers to questions from the audience. Despite his efforts, the museum could not turn a profit, and Rubens lost it to his creditors in 1830.

The building and all it contained were eventually purchased by Barnum, who went on to add other exhibits from competing museums and renamed them all the American Museum. Outwardly, he promised that the enterprise would be educational, advertising that his collection would serve as an "encyclopedia synopsis of everything worth seeing in this curious world." Privately, he began the search for the sort of spectacle which would bring in the crowds that Rubens had struggled to attract.

The competition was fierce. A German immigrant by the name of Albert Carl Koch toured Manhattan with the mounted bones of what appeared to be an enormous sea serpent nearly 120 feet long. Only after the specimen was exhibited in Boston and newspapers suggested that it was the remains of a beast that had escaped from Noah's Ark did several Harvard scholars examine it. They concluded that it was simply a jumbled arrangement of fossilized whale bones purporting to be a much larger animal.

Not to be outdone, Barnum purchased the black, shriveled

body of what was said to be a "FeeJee Mermaid" that had been caught off the coast of Japan toward the end of the nineteenth century. Three feet long, with sharp teeth and scaly skin, the specimen had in fact been masterfully stitched together using parts from a baboon, an orangutan, and a shark, among other creatures. Barnum knew that the "all-important question" for audiences was that they be allowed to "see and examine the specimen" to judge the truth for themselves. He exhibited it at the American Museum, bringing in the then-unheard-of sum of $1,000 in revenue the first week the mermaid was on exhibit— three times its normal amount—which cemented its place as the most popular choice of entertainment in New York. The American Museum sold more than 30 million tickets over the next decade, including one to president-elect Abraham Lincoln, who walked past a crowd of 250,000 gawking New Yorkers to view the collection on February 19, 1861, while on a tour of the country before his inauguration. When it burned down five years after Lincoln's visit, Barnum lost interest in museums and turned his attention to a traveling circus that one day would reach Topeka, Kansas, and prompt a young Frank Brown to name his new baby brother after the showman.

Bickmore's American Museum of Natural History, which would be devoted to fusty subjects like rocks and bones, wouldn't have the same instant appeal to the public, so he needed to look elsewhere for funding. He focused on a rising class of millionaires looking to cement their place in society through large donations. This should have been a hard sell, especially with the near-simultaneous founding of the Metropolitan Museum of Art on the other side of Central Park competing for donors. Wealthy Americans at the time felt a keen need to purchase art and other cultural treasures as an outward sign of their sophistication, especially if they were in the rough businesses of railroads or oil.

Yet as industrialization remade the U.S. economy and gave the wealthiest 1 percent of households nearly 25 percent of the country's income, science seemed better equipped to emphasize moral values of discipline, rationality, and the pursuit of knowledge than art, no matter its prestige. It only helped that these priceless scientific gemstones were often discovered while mining the Earth of its material wealth, making them by-products of capitalism.

In its first years in a temporary building in Central Park, the American Museum of Natural History consisted mainly of rare objects of natural origin for patrons to inspect as they "promenaded up and down . . . filling their minds with science, while their ears were filled with the soft strains of Lanner and Strauss," the *New York Times* noted.

Few outside the New York aristocracy were interested in or felt comfortable in such an elite setting. Still, the American Museum of Natural History doubled down on seriousness, building a massive complex of buildings on Central Park West between Seventy-Seventh Street and Eighty-First Street, close to the homes of its benefactors. In 1888, an architect named Josiah Cleveland Cady designed a massive addition featuring so many castle-like towers and turrets that it seemed as if the only thing missing was a moat. The museum began funding explorations across the globe, aspiring to become an elite research institution.

Still, it had to do something to find a way to attract a broad audience. Bickmore began offering free lectures to the city's schoolteachers in hopes that their enthusiasm would spread to their students. At the same time, the museum made an open

A view of the American Museum from the newly opened Dakota Building in 1880. The museum would eventually grow to encompass twenty-six interconnected buildings spanning four city blocks.

appeal to those who felt more at home in P. T. Barnum's dime museum by buying a remarkably lifelike diorama showing an Arab courier on a camel trying to fight off a Barbary lion that was tearing its claws into the camel's side. (In 2017, CT scans and an X-ray revealed that the reason the courier looked so realistic was that its head was a real human skull covered in plaster, most likely stolen from a graveyard.) Once installed in the American Museum, the diorama shared space near the front door with some of the largest fossils in the museum's collection—including a seven-foot-tall Irish elk, a twelve-foot-tall specimen of the flightless giant moa, and a mastodon with impressive tusks.

For all its good intentions, attendance continued to disappoint. One curator made plain what was needed—dinosaurs. They would be the perfect match between the thrilling attractions that the public wanted to see and the responsible exhibits that the museum had to offer. The idea was that a visitor, drawn in by the bones of giant beasts, would stick around and see what else could be found in a sprawling palace of science.

The question was how to fill the museum's empty shelves. When he took the job heading the Department of Vertebrate Paleontology, Osborn pledged that he would turn the museum into a "center for exhibition, publication, and research" in a field "in which America leads the world." The future of the American Museum was effectively in Osborn's hands—the first true challenge of his life.

His offers to buy specimens from both Marsh and Cope were rebuffed, leaving him in the unfamiliar position of competing in a fair fight with museums in other cities. So Osborn hired as his primary assistant Jacob L. Wortman, who had collected for Cope, even though Osborn was a vicious antisemite. And in the new role of preparator, he hired Adam Hermann, who had previously worked for Marsh, to ensure that fossils would not crumble once excavated from stone. Over time, Hermann developed techniques, such as the use of hot glue and plaster, to preserve fossils that are still used to this day. To capture the public imagination until fossil mounts were ready, Osborn brought in artist Charles R. Knight to paint murals showing the prehistoric world. He was betting that displays combining showmanship with paleontology would resurrect public interest in the American Museum.

Within two years, Osborn had collectors in the American West searching for dinosaur fossils. Though they met with little success, Osborn presented a plan to the museum's trustees to open a new Hall of Fossil Reptiles that would make the museum "the world's leading center for fossil reptiles," despite having nothing to display in it. He was desperate to find the bones that would salvage his reputation and safeguard the good opinion of his father. For all of his willingness to fund his son's life, William Henry Osborn demanded that his son's scientific career "maintain the family prestige."

CHAPTER SIX

A REAL ADVENTURE

Barnum Brown had to read the life-changing letter from the American Museum of Natural History twice, unable to get past the fact that it had come from New York City—a place so foreign that it may as well have been on the moon. In the letter, Jacob Wortman offered Brown a spot on the museum's field expedition that summer. If he accepted, he would need to meet up with the party somewhere in the western states by a certain date. Everything beyond that—his destination or the expedition's ultimate aim—was a mystery. While most people would have a list of questions before committing themselves to a dangerous, months-long expedition, Brown saw only answered prayers. He immediately withdrew from his classes at the University of Kansas and moved out of Professor Williston's home.

Brown learned that the expedition was to start the summer of 1896 in the San Juan Basin in northwestern New Mexico. The land was a parched high desert landscape of bleached rocks and ravines that millennia ago had been a white-sand beach along the shore of a sea covering what is now eastern Utah. As the water receded and tectonic plates shifted, the area became a floodplain where animal carcasses were often covered in sediment before they had the chance to be destroyed by scavengers, providing the right conditions for the slow process of fossilization to begin. Osborn sent the expedition to the unforgiving terrain in search of the remains of early mammals. Once found, he planned to feature the specimens in an exhibit showing the course of evolution immediately following the disappearance of dinosaurs. This would put the museum at the center of the investigation searching for why these later animals never reached the immense size of the extinct dinosaurs.

Osborn particularly hoped to find a skull of a *Coryphodon*, a hoofed mammal roughly the size of a cow that was one of the first large mammals to appear after an asteroid hit the Yucatán Peninsula in what is now Mexico about 65 million years ago. The asteroid killed an estimated 80 percent of all animal life on Earth, wiping away all dinosaur species that did not evolve to become what we know now as birds.

Like all expeditions, the crew balanced the competing demands of money and time. Each day in the field that did not result in a museum-quality fossil was a day wasted. Though the museum had few specimens of its own, Osborn refused to put anything on the exhibition floor that did not meet his exacting standards. Wortman and his crew lived with the constant fear that Osborn would revoke their funding and spend it elsewhere. Yet the appeal of being associated with a museum based in New York and its funding were hard to pass up.

The wagon train set off from Colorado in extremely cold mid-April weather and remained in the Badlands as the season turned and the sun scalded them in June. Each day fell into the same cycle of blasting, digging, and disappointment. "After a month's hard work, under the most trying circumstances, we found ourselves with practically no results," Wortman wrote.

The youngest member of the team, Brown, proved that he not only had the physical endurance to withstand the grueling extremes of weather but the social skills to make it all seem like a grand adventure. He began trading supplies with a Native American family who lived near the dig site, offering cornmeal for fresh goat milk.

By late June, the weather was too hot to continue in New Mexico. The expedition had found several mammalian fossils, but no *Coryphodon*. Unwilling to waste an entire prospecting season, Osborn directed Wortman to buy a wagon and head north. Over the next few weeks, the expedition party trudged seven hundred miles to a remote quarry in the Bighorn Basin of Wyoming. Everything necessary for survival—food, guns, bullets, and barrels of water—had to be planned and accounted for, given that there were no lifelines to help if the party became stranded. It was as if they were walking off the corner of the map and into the great unknown, while expecting to bring back evidence of unreal creatures that lived in a world unrecognizable as our own.

The party reached their destination on July 18. They spent the next six weeks collecting in a desolate region with topography that rose to a high point of more than 11,000 feet quickly falling to a valley nearly 8,000 feet lower. This exposed layers of rock that in some places were more than 2.5 billion years old. Wortman had been the first known paleontologist to explore the region nineteen years earlier, while collecting for Cope.

Through hard effort, Wortman had learned that what he called blue beds—limestone nodules tinted dark blue by oxidation—were the most likely to hold fossils. He discovered three previously unknown extinct mammalian species in his first season exploring the region. Now he returned to the blue beds with his American Museum team. Over the following weeks, the crew found the remains of extinct horses, monkeys, and a wolverine-like carnivorous mammal known as a creodont, but a *Coryphodon* remained elusive—until Brown unearthed a nearly complete skeleton with a perfect skull, lacking only the hind limbs.

Wortman instantly recognized that it would be the crown jewel of the exhibition, delivering exactly what Osborn demanded. Having found what they needed, Wortman's expedition began their journey back to New York before the weather turned deadly. Brown, however, remained in Laramie through October, trying to find unknown fossil beds that would convince the American Museum or one of its competitors to bring him on as a full-time collector.

Brown's ambition was justified. Not far away lay the quarry where Arthur Lakes and William Reed had found the first known *Stegosaurus* in the remote outcrops at Como Bluff years before. Though Marsh had paid him a paltry $50 for the whole quarry, Reed grew to be fanatically loyal to him. He even dynamited the fossils he left behind so they would not fall into Cope's hands. Later, fed up with the low pay and Marsh's domineering nature, Reed quit prospecting. He spent more than a decade bouncing among jobs, until the early 1890s, when the University of Wyoming decided to establish its own collection of vertebrate fossils to keep local discoveries in the state. Reed was hired at a salary of $1,000 per year and the university soon announced that its "bone room" was as large as the collection at Yale.

While in Wyoming, Brown befriended Reed and learned of potentially rich, untapped deposits. He shared this information with Wortman at the American Museum, hoping to prove himself useful enough to be called back for another season of work. He then returned to Lawrence in mid-November, where he jumped back into his coursework. Still, it was hard not to find himself daydreaming of pulling a fossil out of a canyon or gully.

That spring, Brown received his first letter directly from Osborn. Though careful not to offer any outright promises, Osborn dangled the lure of New York City and a possible scholarship to Columbia University. In exchange, he wrote, "I would like a report from you regarding the Jurassic mammal beds, and although I would like you to talk over your plans with Professor Williston, for several reasons I prefer that you should not speak to anyone else about them."

Brown completed the report within a week and sent it to New York, his excitement at the possibility of heading back to Wyoming burning so hot that it could have been felt in New York itself. Though Osborn had not formally offered him a job that summer, Brown prepared himself to head back out into the field and hoped that this time he would lead an expedition himself. He wrote to Osborn, "I am deeply grateful for your kind offer. The University and Museum work is exactly what I desire." Brown then detailed his proposal to prospect for the specimens that Osborn craved: dinosaurs. "As to the reptiles," Brown wrote, "I worked with Mr. Reed a few days in a quarry west of Laramie where the bones were literally packed one on top of the other, nearly all in a good state of preservation."

It was exactly what Osborn wanted to hear.

At the turn of the twentieth century, the forces of industrialization and the rise of corporations created wealth on a scale never before seen for a handful of men. For them, collecting great art would no longer be enough. Something far rarer and more difficult would be necessary to showcase the power and wealth of these new gilded tycoons, who were able to sway millions of lives around the world with their decisions. Nothing less than acquiring and displaying fossils of dinosaurs—the largest and most powerful beasts to ever walk the Earth—could mirror their status in life. And only the discovery of dinosaur bones in the American West that were more gigantic than anything previously imagined could truly reflect the oversized influence of the men whose money made the discoveries possible.

At a time when the gulf between the well-off and the rest of the country had grown wider than ever before, the super-rich tried to hold off criticism of their immense wealth by convincing people that funding natural history museums benefitted everyone by expanding opportunities for public education. But filling these museums often proved harder in practice than in theory. What good would donating hundreds of thousands of dollars to a museum do if the exhibits weren't spectacular and no one showed up?

Osborn knew that he needed large dinosaur fossils to accomplish this goal, but during one of the greatest challenges in his life, his money and his connections had let him down. Thanks to Brown, however, he had unexpectedly found a connection to the same valuable bone quarries that had once built Marsh's reputation. Brown was unproven; the fossil beds, however, were not. So Osborn wrote to Brown, offering to back a small prospecting trip that summer. Brown jumped at the opportunity, setting off into the wilderness with his future—and that of the museum—resting on his young shoulders.

Brown returned to Laramie in early May, intending to retrace Reed's steps to the quarry. Within days he was in over his head. The roads were a mess; supplies were virtually unobtainable; hiring others to help seemed impossible. Worse yet, the information he had gathered from Reed had proven hopelessly out of date, making him feel as if he had been caught in a lie that would destroy his career before it had even begun. Not knowing what else to do, he wrote a long letter to Osborn.

"I feel pretty badly mixed up in the situation, that I have misinformed you somewhat," he wrote in a rambling letter, describing the sorry state of the quarry he had hoped to reopen. His fear of disappointing Osborn immobilized him, with each pang of doubt reaffirming his insecurity that he was a college kid out of his depth. In time, Brown would become legendary for his cool wit and gregarious nature. Yet at that moment he was still on the border between boyhood and manhood and wanted nothing more than for someone to show him the way. He wrote, "I don't know how much expense I dare take on myself or what other things might present themselves to your mind. Wire me immediately what to do."

Forty-eight hours later, Brown regained his confidence and wrote another letter to Osborn, his thoughts of self-doubt washed away. "There are certainly other mammal beds there and plenty of reptile material. Shall I not collect everything?" In what surely appealed to Osborn's social and religious codes, Brown's solution was simply to work harder, trusting that his seemingly innate ability to discover fossils would clear any obstacle.

Brown left Laramie in early May for Como Bluffs, which had

an outcropping dating back approximately 150 million years, when the sagebrush prairie he saw around him was once a humid subtropical plain. It was during this period, known as the late Jurassic, that dinosaurs began expanding to larger and larger sizes. Paleontologists still do not know why. One theory is that dinosaur bones grew hollower, like those of birds, making them weigh significantly less than a solid-boned mammal of similar proportions. This would allow dinosaurs to balloon over tens of millions of years before reaching their peak size during the Cretaceous period.

Sixty-five million years later, Brown trekked out through the remnants of a once-fertile landscape, hoping to uncover the largest bones he could find. He spent the first weeks of the summer opening one of Marsh's former mammal quarries. Brown worked alone, sifting through the rock and dirt for something that would make Osborn's trust in him seem warranted. He could not help but notice an adjacent quarry that had once been tapped by collectors working for Cope. When he came up empty-handed in the Marsh quarry, Brown shifted over to the Cope one. Nearly as soon as he began digging he found dinosaur fossils, so many that he knew there was no way he could excavate them all by himself. The quarry was a "veritable gold mine and I have bones up to my eyes," Brown wrote in a letter to Osborn. Unable to resist seeing it for himself, Osborn left on a rare trip into the field as soon as Brown's message reached him.

There, in the Badlands of Wyoming, Brown and Osborn met face-to-face for the first time. They had no way of knowing that their fates would become so closely stitched that the success of one would not be possible without the other. The bond between them would grow over time, yet it would forever be rooted in the fear of failure that each man recognized in the other. In a photo taken that summer, Osborn and Brown are posed high on a bluff with barren hills behind them. Between them, sticking out of the rock like a rat's tail, lies a three-foot-long bone of a *Diplodocus*, which would soon become the first dinosaur specimen in the museum's collection.

Everything about the specimen was big. Its teeth were the size of pencils, each foot larger than a grown man. An adult *Diplodocus longus* stretched up to ninety-two feet long, making it not only one of the longest sauropods—a group of dinosaurs so named for their graceful, extended necks—but one of the longest animals in the history of Earth. Its two-foot-long head was connected to a neck that could stretch more than twenty-one feet, while its tail spanned another forty-five feet behind it. A third of the tail tapered to a thin tip, known as its whiplash, which paleontologists believe the animal cracked to intimidate predators and possibly communicate with other members of its herd. Though immense, *Diplodocus* was strangely light for its size. At fifteen tons, it weighed about half that of comparable sauropods and less than a tenth of a blue whale.

With one exposed bone and hopes for a full skeleton beneath it, Brown and Osborn stood at what would be the start of a very complicated puzzle. A full dinosaur specimen would guarantee that crowds would come to any institution where it was displayed. A random leg or arm bone or a scattering of teeth, meanwhile, would be of intense interest to paleontologists but make no ripples on a museum floor. Osborn realized within a few days that the process would take weeks, far more time on the frontier than he could stand. Before he left, he sent messages to Wortman, who was then prospecting in Colorado, and a field crew working in Nebraska to abandon their projects and rush to Wyoming. Not long after he arrived, Wortman discovered another giant fossil while attempting to excavate the *Diplodocus*. The new specimen was an *Apatosaurus*, which when alive had stretched seventy-five feet long and stood on four massive, pillarlike legs.

The work continued through the heat of August. Wortman and the crew of reinforcements worked on the *Apatosaurus*. Brown took on the *Diplodocus* alone, covering each exposed portion of the skeleton in a jacket of plaster. Dozens of crates

Well before they knew their lives would be integrally intertwined, Brown and Osborn met in the Badlands of Wyoming when Brown uncovered the bones of a *Diplodocus*, the first dinosaur specimen in the American Museum's collection.

filled with wrapped bones were loaded onto trains heading east as the prospecting season wound down in September, the freight cost of shipping tons of fossils paid for by a connection of Osborn's father.

With their first dinosaur specimens in hand, Osborn published a report in which he inserted the fact that he had been the co-discoverer of the two specimens uncovered that summer. "They are, perhaps, by far, the most complete and perfect of their kind that have ever been collected and will make magnificent material for purposes of exhibition," he wrote. He sketched out plans for two freestanding displays that would mount the creatures in lifelike poses, a feat that had never before been attempted with fossils so large. The dinosaurs would validate his big dreams for the American Museum and be a monument to his genius.

For Brown, meanwhile, the adventure was only beginning. Toward the end of the summer, Osborn informed him in a terse letter that he had been selected for the full scholarship to Columbia University. He had braved the wilderness. Now his prize was waiting for him: New York City.

CHAPTER SEVEN

FINDING A PLACE IN THE WORLD

I n the late summer of 1897, Barnum Brown stepped off a train from Kansas into one of the busiest stations in the world. A few months after Brown arrived in the city, more than ten thousand people in Union Square braved a bitter New Year's Eve rain to watch a parade of electric floats celebrating the Festival of Connection, honoring the joining of Manhattan, Brooklyn, Queens, the Bronx, and Staten Island into the modern City of New York. At midnight the nation's first- and fourth-largest cities became one super-metropolis, a giant with a footprint stretching nearly 303 square miles.

Everywhere Brown looked were signs of the modern era overtaking the past. In lower Manhattan, Trinity Church's fifty-year reign as Manhattan's tallest structure, at 281 feet, would soon end. A few blocks away workers were clearing Revolutionary War–era stables and stores for the new Park Row Building, whose 391-foot twin domes would take the crown when completed in 1899.

Brown was one of millions of new arrivals to the city, many coming, like him, from small or rural towns and driven by the chance at a better life. More than 1.5 million immigrants had passed through Ellis Island over the previous ten years, willing to brave the unknown. Nearly 100,000 African Americans from the South migrated to New York over the same period, finding a foothold of freedom within memory of the abolition of slavery.

Those riding the swelling fortunes of Wall Street made their homes in grand new apartment buildings that stood as shrines to the new era of money. While the rich moved higher into the sky, more than 2.3 million people—two-thirds of the city's population—crammed into squalid tenements downtown, barely able to survive. The poverty of the growing city, especially among its youngest residents, pushed social reformers to call for playgrounds, parks, schools—anything that would offer a citizen of the slums a glimmer of life beyond their narrow horizons.

The American Museum was one of the few places that could potentially unite the city's rich and poor, bringing them together through a shared fascination with the natural world. For that to happen, the museum had to find a way to bring in more visitors. So far, nothing was working. Despite all of its efforts, the museum staff had accomplished the impossible: making a collection of some of the rarest and most fascinating items ever collected seem boring and unworthy of a person's time.

Though the museum had the skeletons of the *Diplodocus* and the *Apatosaurus* unearthed in Wyoming, it would take months if not years to prepare them for display. Everything about paleontology was slow at a time when the museum needed a hit right away. With no dinosaur fossils ready to show, Osborn filled the halls of the Vertebrate Paleontology wing with large charts showing the succession of animals found in rock layers in North America and watercolor landscapes. His main attraction was the skeleton of a three-toed rhinoceros. He knew that it was not enough.

As Brown walked through the museum's halls for the first time, he passed through empty rooms earmarked to hold bones that he had not yet found. He knew, more than anyone, how an exposure to science at a young age could change the course of a life, and he felt the weight of finding attractions that could hold the interest of children like him. He had already traveled farther from Carbondale than he had dared to imagine, yet it only made him realize that the world was bigger than his childhood dreams.

He began a new routine, living in a room of a house on East Sixty-Seventh Street, working at the museum as an assistant curator of vertebrate paleontology, and taking graduate courses at Columbia, though he had not yet completed his bachelor's degree from the University of Kansas. Unlike his fellow students, Brown was there for the education and the increase in rank it would signal rather than for the connections he might make. The stiff, slow world of formal education did not excite him, and he soon fell behind, daydreaming about another dig rather than the slog of completing another paper.

In the field, Brown would have outshone every other student. Yet the skills that helped so much on the frontier—a willingness to try anything, to bend the rules, and to rely on physical strength and endurance to outlast any competitors—were of no use in a lecture hall. He longed for the adventure of discovering the fossils that would form the basis of ideas his fellow classmates were now discussing. He belonged to the paleontology of dirt and rocks and dust, and instead was asked to make do in a world of paper and books and pencils.

The classroom could also not compete with the appeal of a

beautiful woman. Marion Raymond was a part-time graduate student at Columbia, finishing her master's degree while teaching high school biology. She was the daughter of a distinguished lawyer and educator from Oxford, New York, a woman most comfortable with a book or in a laboratory. Brown was a farmer's son who, despite his brilliance and long career, would write only two scientific papers and could never stand to stay in one place for long. Yet something about the two clicked, each finding in the other what they had been missing in themselves. As Barnum and Marion began spending long hours in each other's worlds, he experienced the unusual sensation of slowing down and talking with a woman whose mind equaled his own, while she grew comfortable with the pleasant chaos that was Barnum's drive to experience all that the world had to offer.

For the first time in his life, Barnum began to feel his restlessness seep away and contentment sprout. Before Marion, before New York, before the museum, he had always felt the need to chase something down. Now he held a job that was his childhood fantasy while living in a city as different from the farm back home as he could imagine. And he felt himself falling in love for the first time. For a man who could never feel peace, his world was finally settling into place.

And that was when Osborn came into his office one morning and told him to pack his bags for Patagonia.

CHAPTER EIGHT

THE MOST EXTREME PLACE ON EARTH

The Patagonia region of South America sits at the southernmost point of the continent, extending over 900,000 square miles through Argentina and Chile. Sandwiched between two oceans, a strait, and a river, its interior offers a variety of the Earth's extremes: mountainous peaks where sudden violent snowstorms appear without warning give way to nearly barren deserts marked by deep gorges. Lush forests taper into the largest ice fields in the Southern Hemisphere outside of Antarctica. The region ends in an archipelago that Spanish explorers named Tierra del Fuego, or Land of Fire. There, hundred-foot waves routinely batter boats trying to round Cape Horn, leaving its shores a graveyard of ships and sailors alike.

In 1832, a ninety-foot-long ship called the HMS *Beagle* had appeared off the cape while on a five-year-long voyage around the world. Among the sixty-eight men on board was twenty-four-year-old Charles Darwin. He paid his own way to serve as the voyage's naturalist, intent on collecting and cataloging plants and animals unseen by English eyes.

Darwin was decades away from formulating the theory of evolution by natural selection that would make him a pillar of

British science. He spent the entire five-year journey battling violent seasickness, heaving with each passing swell. When he was not seasick, Darwin drew in the richness and variety of ocean life. He noticed the subtle artistry in oyster shells embedded in rocks and the gracefulness of tiny fish and plankton he pulled up in his net, all the while wondering why God spent time perfecting something so few people would see. "Many of these creatures so low in the scale of nature are most exquisite in their forms & rich colours," he wrote. "It creates a feeling of wonder that so much beauty should be apparently created for such little purpose."

Each day he encountered another mystery of nature and plunged headlong into trying to figure it out. When at sea, he formulated theories as to how coral reefs formed. When on land, he wanted to collect every animal in the jungle. After nearly a year at sea, the *Beagle* reached Patagonia. The solitude of the landscape unnerved Darwin, and he spent his hours on watch painfully aware of how far away he was from home.

The expedition spent the winter in Patagonia, giving Darwin a chance to explore the rivers leading up to the Andes. There, he collected samples of everything he could find. He began to realize that the undeveloped region was in fact a giant graveyard, filled with the bones of enormous animals that no longer inhabited the Earth. Patagonia was "a perfect catacomb for monsters of extinct races," he marveled. He found huge prehistoric armadillos and giant birds, all the while wondering why some life forms had apparently shrunk over geological time. "It is impossible to reflect on the changed state of the American continent without the deepest astonishment," he wrote. "Formerly it must have swarmed with great monsters: now we find mere pygmies. . . . What has exterminated so many species?"

Darwin would ponder how and why some life forms survived and others did not for decades. Finally, more than twenty years after the *Beagle* expedition ended, Darwin published *On the Origin of Species*, an explanation of evolution driven by natural selection that suddenly made everything from the colors of a peacock's feathers to the colossal bones uncovered in Patagonia make sense.

Among scientists, the region would have remained best associated with Darwin's expedition had it not been for an Argentine paleontologist by the name of Florentino Ameghino. The self-educated son of Italian immigrants, Ameghino first discovered natural history through books, and then through long walks in his adopted country. His genius was apparent despite his poverty, and he eventually became a professor of geology and mineralogy at the University of La Plata. There he found himself embroiled in the most burning question of the era: if Darwin's theory of evolution through natural selection was indeed correct, then how and where did humans and other mammals originate?

While European and American scientists centered their view on Africa, Ameghino argued in a well-publicized paper that Argentina was the cradle of human life. His theory drew fierce criticism from European scientists, but others found it credible enough that expedition teams from around the world set out to Argentina to investigate. Cope, for his part, called the paper "a monumental work."

Osborn lived for any chance to make the American Museum part of an intellectual debate to further his own reputation. Ameghino's theory proved especially difficult for him to pass up, since Osborn had long doubted that humankind originated from a common ancestor in Africa. Over time, his suspicion would harden into something crueler, infused with the vile notion that light-skinned Europeans were naturally smarter and stronger than dark-skinned Africans. Osborn's racism was common among his peers; however, he took this a step further. Rather than viewing skin tone as just one of many adaptations that evolve in a species over generations, he suggested that light-skinned humans did not evolve from apes but from some other species yet to be discovered in a parallel evolution. Throughout his life, Osborn never wavered in his refusal to accept that a common thread of humanity lay below the veneer of skin color. His racism would infect the American Museum of Natural History, leading to displays and exhibitions that implied that white Protestants of what Osborn called the Nordic race were the pinnacle of billions of years of evolution.

As those theories hardened in his head, he struck a deal to send Brown along on a trip organized by his college friend William Berryman Scott, to search for clues to mammalian evolution in Patagonia. If Brown could find a *Diplodocus* alone, then who knows what he would bring back from a region known for its abundant fossils. The decision infuriated Jacob Wortman, who had lobbied hard to be given the opportunity himself. Passed over for a man barely out of college who had served as his trainee not long before, Wortman began nursing a grudge against Brown that he held on to for the rest of his life.

Brown knew nothing of Osborn's plans when he arrived at the American Museum shortly before nine in the morning on December 7, 1898. "Before I had taken my hat off, Professor Osborn called me into his office," Brown later wrote, describing the two-minute conversation that upended his life. Osborn asked him, "Brown, I want you to go to Patagonia today with the Princeton expedition. . . . The boat leaves at eleven; will you go?" Without hesitation, Brown replied, "This is short notice, Professor Osborn, but I'll be on that boat."

Brown rushed home, packed a small bag, and raced to board the Grace Line freighter named the *Capac* for a nonstop voyage of over six thousand miles to the port of Punta Arenas on the Strait of Magellan. As the ship left New York Harbor, Brown found himself yet again in an alien environment. It was his first time at sea, and he "soon was a victim of seasickness, first hoping [he] would die, and then afraid [he] wouldn't," Brown later wrote. For thirty days, the ship steadily moved south. Christmas and New Year's Day passed by, two days spent like any other staring out at the featureless ocean.

The *Capac* finally reached Punta Arenas in early January, and its crew rushed to gather provisions for the expedition ahead, like squirrels surprised by an early snowfall. The expedition's leader, John Bell Hatcher, directed his men to stock up on enough food, shovels, pickaxes, and whiskey to last for several months. He acquired two teams of horses and harnessed them to a cloth-covered wagon. This would be the first time that a scientific expedition attempted to cross the vast, windswept Patagonian pampas on a set of wheels.

Hatcher jumped on the back of a horse and rode ahead alone to check on the condition of a fossil bed he had uncovered the previous spring. Brown and another assistant followed behind on a four-hundred-mile route along smooth, flat stones that had once been covered by the receding ocean. A few days into the trip, Brown was holding the reins when the ground around them began to fall sharply, as if a plug had been pulled from below. He yanked the horses as hard as he could to the side and tried to race ahead, not knowing whether the land itself was crumbling. When he looked back, he realized that the wagon had barely escaped falling into a deep, quicksand-like bog of mud known as a soap hole. "Had the team and wagon gone into this mass, we would have all gone down without anyone knowing where we had disappeared," Brown wrote, spooked at the realization that he was crossing a place where even the ground seemed out to get him.

They reached the foothills of the Andes and began the slow trek upward. Once the trail became impassable, they ditched their wagon on a dry lakebed and continued on horseback. Finally, in March, Brown reunited with Hatcher. The expedition team was almost immediately caught in a blizzard, forcing them to release their horses to seek shelter. Brown, Hatcher, and the others crammed onto one single bed in a tent and remained there for two days to conserve body heat. The storm eventually passed, allowing a brief window of time to dig before another sudden violent snowstorm again whipped through, halting everything once more.

Hatcher's calm demeanor while battling the weather made an impression on the twenty-five-year-old Brown. While Osborn's wealth and status would forever make him a man apart, Hatcher was someone whom Brown found himself looking up to as a mentor. He admired how Hatcher carried himself with a sense of purpose. Furthermore, he had demonstrated an ability, which Brown had not yet mastered, to mesh the scientific world of papers and lectures with the real-life skill to acquire ground-breaking fossils. Brown had already shown his worth outside of the classroom, yet he still doubted whether his academic skills would ever catch up. Hatcher was "a truly remarkable man," Brown would later write. "He would ride off alone in an uncharted area, with only his blankets, revolver, and a pocket full of salt, living off the game of the land as he travelled."

After two months and several snowstorms, Hatcher had to admit that the trip was proving to be a bust. The fossil beds he had expected to find in abundance were nearly nonexistent. He announced that the expedition would return to Punta Arenas and head home. They descended from the mountains, their empty wagon reminding them of their failures with each easy rotation of its wheels.

While Hatcher consulted with travel agents for the next ocean liner to New York, Brown explored nearby marine beds, unable to stand the thought of disappointing Osborn so thoroughly. By chance, he found the skull, jaw, and vertebrae of a toothed whale that had lived in the Miocene, some 5 million years ago. It was enough to keep him from getting on the boat home. Brown had never come home empty-handed from the field, and he did not want to start now. As Hatcher and the other members of the expedition boarded the ship, Brown was far away, gathering supplies for what would become a six-month mission prospecting alone along the coast of South America. With no one to answer to, he allowed himself to get lost in the natural world, his ambition and curiosity pushing him to take risks that older, more experienced prospectors would never dare.

At Cañon de las Vacas, he built a sling out of a tarp and used it to hang off a cliff face so that he could chisel out what turned out to be an armadillo-like creature known as a *Propaleohoplophorus*. This specimen now stands in the American Museum's Hall of Mammals and Their Extinct Relatives. Near the outlet where the Gallegos River spills into the Atlantic, he dodged incoming waves and the occasional shark to dig up a fossil exposed at low tide. After several hours of work, he pulled out the skull and jaw of an extinct creature known as an *Astrapotherium*, which looked like a cross between an elephant and a hippopotamus yet was unrelated to either.

By October, Brown had amassed an impressive haul of fossils. Over six months of solitude, he had confronted one of the most treacherous regions on the planet and walked away with a greater trust in himself and his path in life. While he did not have wealth like Osborn, and had not yet discovered a major species like Hatcher, he had tested himself in a grand arena and left its stage pleased with the results. That his finds had come after a man he looked up to as a mentor decided to give up only sweetened the triumph.

His time in Patagonia had made clear what he knew all along: he was not meant to be an academic, with one foot in the classroom and one in the field. He was built for a life of action, as comfortable in the roughest terrain in the world as he was in Greenwich Village.

Today, several specimens that Brown collected on his solitary expedition in Patagonia remain on display on the floor of the American Museum. Alone in the wild, Brown faced down his self-doubt and now looked forward to rejoining his life in New York and the possibility of reestablishing a relationship with Marion, if she remembered him. If she did not, then the trip was still worth it.

The next scheduled ship to New York was several weeks

away. Hearing of his predicament, the captain of a ship heading to Portugal offered Brown a ride across the Atlantic. There, perhaps, he could find a quicker connection to New York. Brown soon found himself in Paris and London, examining the collections of what were considered the best natural history

Brown always hoped to become the cosmopolitan adventurer of his childhood dreams. Here he is shown wearing a fur coat while on a dig in Sweetwater, Montana, in 1914.

museums in the world, the dirt from his digs in Patagonia still clinging to his boots. By the time Brown finally returned to New York, he had shed all markers of the farm boy he once was. "He bought an entire new outfit in Paris, including a tall, collapsible silk hat," his daughter would later write. "Sporting a moustache and a pointed Vandyke beard, he then considered himself the epitome of a cultured European."

For the rest of his life, Brown brought a suit, tie, and full-length beaver fur coat on digs, often looking more the part of a man ready to drop into an opera than a scrappy paleontologist. It was as if he was trying to will away those hours of suffocation and containment on the farm by becoming the flamboyant explorer of his boyhood dreams. That self-possession would soon meet its gravest challenge, however, as Brown realized upon his return how much New York—and indeed, his standing at the museum—had changed in his absence.

CHAPTER NINE

BIG THINGS

B rown watched the towers of Lower Manhattan grow larger as the steamship carrying him back from Europe passed through the Verrazano Narrows on June 10, 1900. He had been gone for sixteen months, and in that time the promise of New York had only grown. Its riches were larger, its population greater, its possibilities wilder. It was the jewel of the world's fastest-growing economy, drawing the most talented and ambitious of a young nation. Nowhere else was the link between science and wealth as highly regarded, and nowhere else were the profits of an economy built on industry and machinery displayed as lavishly.

Skyscrapers soared and mansions bloomed, each one a new ornament to prosperity. The American Museum was among them, an intellectual cathedral carved from the city's wealth. Brown looked forward to spending several months reacquainting himself with the museum's collection and making space for the specimens he had collected over his long absence. And in his personal life, he planned to contact Marion, hoping that their relationship could rekindle after a long period of silence.

Within weeks, however, he was in the Badlands of South Dakota and Wyoming.

Nearly as soon as Brown stepped off the boat, he found himself well behind in a race that he did not know had begun. Four years earlier, William Reed had helped Brown locate the fossil beds where he uncovered the American Museum's *Diplodocus*, and asked for nothing in return. Since then, through Reed's work, the University of Wyoming built a collection of dinosaur fossils that rivaled any on the East Coast, putting contentment within Reed's grasp after a lifetime of chasing dreams.

What the university did not have, however, was money. Reed had helped create a new economy dealing in large bones. He ultimately could not settle for a regular paycheck when there was the chance for a large payday. "Our university is so poor that I am thinking of leaving it and selling my fossils in Europe or to some other American museum. . . . The bones here are no. 1 in quality and some of them are monsters," Reed confided in a letter to Marsh, hoping to spark his interest in a big buy. Marsh was in no position to take Reed up on the offer since his funding had dried up due to his behavior in the Bone Wars, but Reed wasn't ready to give up.

Invitations to tour his workshop and marvel at his discoveries soon reached newspaper reporters in every city with a major museum. The *New York Journal* devoted a full page to announcing that "Most Colossal Animal Ever on Earth Just Found Out West." The article appeared on December 11, 1898, just four days after Brown left for Patagonia. A portrait of Reed standing next to a *Brontosaurus* femur taller and wider than his own body ran with the article, along with a drawing of what the beast's skeleton would look like when fully assembled. In it, the dinosaur towers over a man standing underneath its belly, the size difference suggesting a dog and one of its ticks.

A copy of the article landed on the desk of Andrew Carnegie, one of the wealthiest men who ever lived. As luck would have it, he was then in the process of trying to fill up a new natural history museum in the town that had made him rich. "Can't you buy this for Pittsburgh?" Carnegie wrote in the margin of a copy of the article he forwarded to the director of the Carnegie Museum of Natural History.

Andrew Carnegie had not always been interested in big things. The son of a handloom weaver and a shoemaker who emigrated from Dunfermline, Scotland, he dreamed as a boy of becoming a bookkeeper. With his uncle's help, he got a job running messages for the O'Reilly Telegraph Company. There, he found that he was comfortable in the often violent and ruthless world of industry and willed himself into a larger life. By the age of twenty-four, he rose to a position as a district manager at the powerful Pennsylvania Railroad.

Stuck with a body whose height did not match his ambition, he began wearing high-heeled boots and a top hat to make himself seem more imposing than his natural five feet suggested. By the age of thirty, he was running his own company and grew rich from now-illegal insider deals. By forty, he controlled steel companies, iron ore mines, oil wells, bond-trading firms, and bridge builders. Carnegie spent his days in a hotel suite in Manhattan, where he worked only a few hours each morning yet reaped unimaginable wealth.

Carnegie was the rare captain of industry who grew tired of

the hunt for profit and tried to shape himself into a man of culture, forging friendships with artists and intellectuals at home and in Europe. In his thirties, he resolved to "make no effort to increase [his] fortune, but spend the surplus each year for benevolent purposes." Philanthropy, he argued, was "the true antidote for the temporary unequal distribution of wealth, the reconciliation of the rich and the poor." Over time, he built 1,689 public libraries in the United States, set up a trust to pay the tuition of Scottish university students, funded pensions for American college professors, established a Hero Fund to award civilians who took extraordinary risks to save another person's life, built a complex of four world-class museums in Pittsburgh, and founded a think tank to promote international peace.

"The man who dies thus rich dies disgraced," he wrote in an essay called "The Gospel of Wealth," published in June 1889. A museum of natural history provided the unique prospect of sparking interest in science among those who couldn't afford formal education, fueling the sort of intellectual self-improvement that Carnegie saw as the key to future prosperity. In a city such as Pittsburgh, bursting with people who worked with their hands, a museum that did not "attract the manual toilers, and benefit them . . . will have failed its mission," he wrote.

Dinosaur bones, especially those so large as to make an adult tremble, were exactly what he needed to bring in the masses and kindle their curiosity about the wider world. With the flame ignited by an exposure to dinosaurs, Carnegie believed he could nudge others along the same path to knowledge that he had once walked.

William Holland, the director of the Carnegie Museum, knew almost nothing about paleontology, having worked as a pastor in

Pittsburgh before turning his attention to entomology. Like his counterpart Osborn at the American Museum, Holland's greatest strength was unwavering self-confidence. Doubt that he was the right person to lead a campaign for dinosaur bones seemed never to enter his mind. He contacted Reed shortly after the article in the *New York Journal* appeared and was told the dinosaur was not for sale. Not long after, however, Reed followed up with a letter saying that the University of Wyoming owned the specimen in the article, but that he personally owned another quarry containing a fossil just as large, if not larger. Sensing his payday had finally come, Reed stressed he was under a time constraint. His success at finding fossils had convinced the Wyoming state legislature to provide more funds to the university to expand its collection, and it would be difficult to turn them down if they offered a fair price. Unless Carnegie acted fast, he would lose his "chance to get this monster," Reed warned.

Holland wrote back at once, laying out exactly what he wanted: "Do you think that it promises to be as perfect, for instance, as the skeleton of the *Brontosaur* which Prof. O. C. Marsh has at Yale? . . . I should like very much to obtain for this Museum a specimen as nearly perfect as possible of one of the huge saurians. . . ." Reed assured Holland that the fossils would prove to be exhibition-worthy. Holland boarded a train to Wyoming and presented Reed with a lucrative offer, which included a three-year contract to join the Carnegie Museum staff. Only after Reed signed the paperwork, however, did he reveal that the University of Wyoming had an ownership stake in the quarry where his prospective dinosaur lay and it was not his to sell outright.

Not wanting to tell the world's richest man that he had been bamboozled, Holland tried to buy his way out of the problem.

He offered the university $2,000 for the fossil but was told that "it is the biggest thing on earth and we think that it is worth a hundred thousand dollars." Holland hired attorneys to try to block the university's claim to the material. He also lobbied the state's governor for help and made a second trip to Wyoming to pay local cowboys for any leads about other fossil outcrops. "We shall ultimately get possession of our coveted monster," Holland wrote.

On a trip to New York to strategize with Carnegie, Holland met Jacob Wortman, then on staff at the American Museum, and spoke with him about the difficulties of fieldwork in Wyoming. Wortman made such a strong impression that Holland offered him a job as a curator at the Carnegie Museum, where he would be free of the overbearing shadow cast by Osborn. Shortly after Wortman accepted, he traveled to Wyoming to check on the quarry holding Reed's find, where he discovered that the university's workers had already removed most of the fossils that Reed had identified and destroyed the rest. Empty-handed, Holland convinced Carnegie to fund their own full team of prospectors to Wyoming in the coming months.

The Carnegie expedition was not the only one descending on Wyoming in the summer of 1899. Aiming to increase travel on one of its least-used routes, the Union Pacific Railroad offered free passage to the state for a limited time to amateur prospecting teams from over two hundred colleges and universities. For a brief instant, paleontology was no longer restricted to those who could afford the costs of travel to the far reaches of the country, thanks to what became known as the Wyoming Fossil Fields

Expedition. For the first time, big-city museums would be tested on an open playing field.

Soon, the wilderness was dotted with those who dreamed of finding dinosaur bones. Some were big museums backed by money. Others were college students hoping that a find could kickstart their career. And there were still others—cowboys, drifters, down-on-their-luck gold miners—who only vaguely knew what a dinosaur was or how you would go about finding one, but joined in the chance to strike it rich.

That summer, the dawning age of science, industry, and professionalization faced off directly against the era of hard living, grit, and luck it was replacing. Prospectors rich and poor descended on Medicine Bow, a desolate town on the plains whose train station, three saloons, and twenty houses were the only permanent structures in the sweeping valley of sagebrush and stone. Ten years earlier, the U.S. Census Bureau had announced that the frontier was closed. Yet there still remained a large gap between what government officials considered settlement and what life was like on the forgotten plain. It was a place where lawlessness could literally land in your lap. Shortly before the paleontologists reached town, Butch Cassidy and the Wild Bunch, a notorious gang of outlaws and bank robbers, held up a train and dynamited its safe, containing what would now be worth more than $1 million, in the mountains outside of Medicine Bow.

The few rooms in Medicine Bow fit for human habitation quickly filled up with Union Pacific workers. Yet still more people came. Trains carrying more than one hundred members of the Fossil Fields Expedition arrived over the span of a few days, including not only prospectors but also support staff like teamsters and cooks and field hands, swelling Medicine Bow's population well past its capacity. Soon, nearly every flat place to sleep under a roof was claimed. A run on the town's general store emptied it of every pickaxe, bag of flour, hammer, and chisel.

Fossil hunters braved the dangers of Medicine Bow because it was close to the Freezeout Mountains. The range is made up of sandstone and shale and hides abundant beds of Jurassic fossils in a layer of rock referred to as the Morrison Formation. Named after the town of Morrison, Colorado, the Morrison Formation dates to about 150 million years ago, when the Badlands of Wyoming, Colorado, and Utah were crisscrossed with rivers, streams, and ponds.

In what was one part science and one part gold rush, teams of prospectors swarmed over the mountains and attempted to claim as many quarry sites as possible without knowing what they held. Those who should have never been in the mountains in the first place soon gave up, overheated and exhausted with nothing to show for it. Others tumbled off rocks or tripped over tree branches, their grand adventure cut short by a broken nose or busted ankle. Success was largely a matter of reading the rocks and matching small variations in color with knowledge of what the rock had once been. Dark gray indicated volcanic lava, which could be safely ignored. Grayish-green rock represented layers of siltstone, which likely had been the bottom of a river or a sandbar—exactly the sort of place where the body of an animal could wash up and become covered in sediment.

Even those who knew how to fend for themselves in the wild often came out empty-handed. Prospectors pushed deeper into the inhospitable terrain, hoping to shake themselves of the dilettantes and the desperate. The days "consisted in 'looking out' as much as one could cover of the rock formations exposed in canyons and gullies, prowling over the weathered slopes, and climbing along the steeper cliffs, watching always for the peculiar colors and forms of weathered bone fragments, following up every trail of fragments to its source, and prospecting cautiously with a light pick or digging chisel to see what, if anything, is left in the rock," wrote William Diller Matthew, a curator at the American Museum who spent three weeks that summer in Wyoming.

The Fourth of July provided one of the few breaks in the monotony of the search. Throughout the big, open states of dinosaur country, the holiday was considered a momentous event, one of the few outward signs that there could be any connection between this rough land and the crammed cities on the coast. While the other members of the Carnegie team had a big party in camp, Reed set off alone to hunt. He found antelope footprints and began tracking the animal. It was then that he noticed a bone sticking out of a rock. He began digging with the small tools he carried with him and realized that he had found something.

The following morning, Reed revealed that he had stumbled upon a section of what appeared to be a *Diplodocus*. The others joined him at the site, and it soon became clear that they were at the start of a major find. Onlookers from competing museums were drawn to the spectacle of watching an eighty-four-foot-long prehistoric beast emerge chisel by chisel. Over the following weeks, the specimen revealed itself to be one of the most complete *Diplodocus* ever found, containing all major bones and a flawless skull. Though he was not personally responsible for uncovering it, Wortman was particularly pleased that the Carnegie team, and not the American Museum, had claimed the most impressive discovery that summer.

When news of Carnegie's find reached New York, Osborn

arranged one of his rare trips to the field. He reached Medicine Bow a few weeks later and rode out on horseback to the quarry site. There, he dressed down Walter Granger, his well-liked and respected field foreman, and second-guessed every decision he had made. Among his worst sins in Osborn's eyes was his decision to focus on a few sites rather than widen his approach and outwork his rivals to the point of exhaustion. The element of luck in Reed's discovery was not lost on Osborn, yet he could not accept that a rival was pulling ahead. The realities of camp life were too rough for him, however, and he left after a week to vacation in Colorado, where he continued to send letters to Granger with new commands.

The summer of 1899 proved to be one of the most influential concentrated efforts to dig out dinosaur bones in the short history of paleontology. The amateur collectors who braved the field thanks to the free rail travel unearthed more than two tons of fossils, scattering specimens to universities and colleges across the country, where they offered many people their first opportunity to see clear evidence of prehistoric life. The Field Museum of Chicago, meanwhile, brought home seventy-five dinosaur bones weighing a collective five tons, including the spine and pelvis of a *Brontosaurus*, twenty-five tail vertebrae from a *Diplodocus*, and the pelvis and foot of a *Creosaurus*, the predator now known as *Allosaurus*. It grew up to thirty-five feet long and may have used its head as a hatchet, slamming it into prey and then ripping off flesh into a mouth filled with backward-curved teeth that prevented anything from escaping. For its efforts in the field, the American Museum amassed 131 bones for its collection, including half of a *Brontosaurus* skeleton. Above them all stood the Carnegie Museum, which left Wyoming with most of the spine, pelvis, skull and eighteen ribs of the prized *Diplodocus*, as well as fossils of marine reptiles that expanded the breadth of its shelves. "We obtained a quantity of material which would have made the mouths of Cope and Marsh water," Holland wrote in a letter to a friend.

For the first time since he pivoted his life to focus on paleontology, Osborn had come in second on a public stage. Though the American Museum had made several important finds, nothing in its haul could compare to the specimens obtained by the Carnegie. What's more, the *Diplodocus* the Carnegie team brought home was both bigger and better preserved than the American Museum's specimen that Brown had discovered two years earlier, leaving what had been one of the most important specimens in the museum's collection diminished in Osborn's eyes.

The relationship between Holland and Wortman deteriorated over the winter of 1899–1900, giving Osborn hope that the threat of the rival Carnegie Museum would fizzle away. Instead, once Wortman left, Holland hired an even more experienced fossil hunter named John Bell Hatcher from Princeton to expand the Carnegie's collection of dinosaur bones. In his first months in his new job, Hatcher realized that the *Diplodocus* specimen uncovered in the summer of 1899 was not just immense but represented a new species. He named it *Diplodocus carnegii* in honor of the museum's founder. In a move that made the discovery sting all the more, Holland asked Osborn as a matter of professional courtesy to confirm Hatcher's interpretation of the find, forcing Osborn to publicly acknowledge another museum's superiority. Holland wasted no time in declaring that the Carnegie Museum would soon put Pittsburgh on the world stage.

As Brown walked into the American Museum after eighteen months away, he knew little of the threat that the Carnegie Museum posed to him or his institution. He had left New York as the hero who'd found the museum's first dinosaur fossil. He returned to learn that his discovery had been eclipsed by a larger, better-preserved specimen of a newly recognized species. It was as if all of Brown's fears had come true at once. He was missing when it mattered the most, and now his work uncovering mammalian fossils in Patagonia seemed inconsequential. Should he not return with a comparable fossil that summer, Brown feared that Osborn would use his ample funding to find someone who could.

Brown set off to the Badlands, hoping to find a *Triceratops* skull that would be fit for exhibition. He landed in the broken prairie of South Dakota, about forty miles west of the small city of Edgemont. There, he tracked streams branching off the Cheyenne River, following the path of a floodplain that existed 66 million years ago through modern-day cattle ranches. Over the following weeks, he found several broken fragments of *Triceratops* skulls, but nothing useful for the museum.

In Patagonia, he'd had the freedom to explore where his curiosity took him. Now he felt the presence of other collectors, even when they were hundreds of miles away. That summer, Hatcher was in Wyoming, where he was focused on not only unearthing the remainder of the immense *Diplodocus* first identified the year before but also on winning Carnegie's limitless funds to beat rivals in the future. In Colorado, meanwhile, Elmer Riggs, a curator at the Field Museum working on a dig near

Grand Junction, uncovered a thigh bone on July 26, 1900, which measured six feet ten inches in length, "longer by eight inches than any limb-bone, recent or fossil, known to the scientific world," he wrote.

After word of Riggs's discovery leaked, newspapers across the country ran articles about what the *Boston Journal* called "The Monster of All Ages." Riggs's work on uncovering the rest of the beast—now known as a *Brachiosaurus*, a giraffe-like sauropod that was one of the few dinosaurs whose forelimbs were longer than its hind legs—became so much of a local attraction that he begged the townspeople to keep it to themselves. Yet the tourists kept on coming, drawn by the slow process of unburying a giant whose existence defied the imagination.

Brown, by comparison, worked alone and in obscurity. He continued his hunt throughout the long summer, covering hundreds of miles on horseback without any significant bones to show for it. Brown wondered whether his long luck had finally run out.

Then, on the first day of September, he uncovered a nearly complete duckbilled specimen the size of a rhinoceros. "It gives me great pleasure to announce to you the discovery of a *Claosaurus*," Brown wrote to Osborn, no doubt hoping that his enthusiasm would hide the fact that it was not as impressive as the discoveries that summer by Hatcher or Riggs. Marsh had discovered the first known *Claosaurus* specimen in Kansas in 1872, diminishing Brown's find in comparison to the newly unearthed monsters in Wyoming. Still, it took him a full month to extract the exhibition-worthy specimen from the sandstone. He then continued to roam the prairie, looking for the elusive *Triceratops* skull Osborn needed to maintain the reputation of the museum in the showdown with titans who saw dinosaur fossils as a chance to prove their superiority to their counterparts in New York. Failure would push Brown one step closer to losing all that he had worked for. He had claimed a foothold in New York, but he knew how precarious that position was.

He remained in the field throughout the fall, despite dropping temperatures. A sudden blizzard interrupted him one day in November, yet he refused to let the seasons hold sway. Osborn, normally content to benefit from the labor of others, told Brown that it was time to return to New York. "I have been fearing the snow storms would overtake you . . . I think you had better pack up and come in as soon as you can."

Still, Brown soldiered on. Thanksgiving passed, and then Christmas, and then New Year's. Finally, a deep freeze in early January convinced him to return to New York. As the wind whipped around him, he loaded thirty boxes of fossils into a train car of the Baltimore and Ohio Railroad. As the train trundled toward New York, Brown consoled himself with the thought that his luck would return in the spring and bring him to the elusive *Triceratops* skull. He had let himself down in the field for the first time in his life, and he hoped that it would be the last.

CHAPTER TEN

A VERY COSTLY SEASON

For the first time in his life, Barnum Brown did not know where he belonged.

He had every reason to feel cast aside. At the start of the 1901 field season, Brown planned to return to South Dakota to redeem himself through the discovery of a *Triceratops* skull. Instead, Osborn ordered him to Flagstaff, Arizona, to assist an expedition that was searching for fossilized pinecones near the Grand Canyon. For dinosaurs, Osborn turned instead to George Reber Wieland, who had worked with Marsh until his death in 1899.

Wieland had the Ivy League degree Brown lacked, which allowed him to interact with Osborn as an equal, and an infectious sense of purpose and confidence. Osborn was so taken with Wieland that he even agreed to pay his steep demand for a salary of $150 per month, nearly double what he paid more experienced collectors. Osborn placed Wieland in charge of the museum's dinosaur expeditions that summer, demoting field collectors who had been with the American Museum for several summers. The change in leadership reflected Osborn's insistence on results worthy of restoring the American Museum—and by extension, his own reputation—to its rightful place atop its competitors.

Wieland took charge of a party that reached the village of Hulett in northeastern Wyoming on May 15. There, he established a makeshift camp on the west side of Devils Tower, a nearly vertical shaft of igneous rock that rises 867 feet above the surrounding forest of ponderosa pines and the nearby Belle Fourche River. The picturesque location was once the seabed of a shallow inland sea that began retreating 195 million years ago, leaving behind bands of dark-red sandstone, maroon siltstone, and gray-green shale that in certain areas date to the Jurassic period, some 135 million years ago. Approximately 50 million years ago, an immense shaft of magma—whether coming from a sudden explosion of a volcano or the slow result of millions of years of erosion—pushed up through the rock layers, leaving Devils Tower, which is sacred to Plains Indians tribes, behind.

Wieland's party found nothing while surveying the immediate vicinity of Devils Tower, undercutting his theory that the shaft of rock would contain fossilized sediment from several different ages and leave plentiful fossils exposed. He expanded the search more than twenty miles downriver, without success.

After two weeks, Wieland turned the party around and built an elaborate camp near the base of Devils Tower in preparation for a visit by Osborn, who was touring all the museum's fossil digs that summer from the luxurious comfort of a private Pullman railroad car complete with a personal attendant and chef. He had to leave that all behind to reach Hulett, however, which remained too remote for modern travel. In Deadwood, South Dakota, Osborn boarded a train he called "as primitive . . . as you ever saw" to head deeper into Wyoming. At the end of the line, he boarded a boxy stagecoach that jostled and bumped as it took him the remaining thirty miles over the Black Hills.

Osborn rarely braved such conditions, but his desperation was increasing.

Wieland was not in camp when he arrived, the sort of unintentional slight that Osborn did not easily forget. Once Wieland returned, he hurried to take Osborn on a tour of potential quarry sites. Each spot showed no evidence that Wieland had blasted or begun stripping off the top layers of soil and rock. Osborn grew enraged at the lack of progress. In full view of the members of the expedition, he warned Wieland that he was not only wasting his valuable time but was putting the future of the American Museum in doubt with a wasteful expedition that had nothing to show for its great expense. Stung by the criticism, Wieland offered to resign on the spot. Osborn refused, unwilling to accept failure. He spent another night in camp, hoping for a miracle, before deciding that he had had enough. He canceled the remaining stops on his tour of the west and headed immediately back to the East Coast.

Osborn searched for a way to fill a hole that seemed to get deeper by the day. The Carnegie Museum had just one multimillionaire to please. Osborn had all of New York's aristocracy, including the recently elected museum patron, John D. Rockefeller, whose Standard Oil monopoly had made him the wealthiest person in the nation's history.

All the museum patrons wanted something to show for their money, a prize that proved the institution they had chosen to support was truly the best in the world. That spring, the museum's department of mineralogy opened a sparkling new exhibit. Tiffany & Co. had originally collected and prepared a stunning display of diamonds, emeralds, and sapphires for the Paris World's Fair, helping to cement its reputation as the premier jeweler in America, if not the world. Once the fair was over, Osborn's uncle

J. P. Morgan purchased the whole collection for the museum to display, which he considered a better use of his money than funding another summer of dinosaur hunts that might turn up nothing. The difficulty of finding huge dinosaur bones led him to question whether there really were other specimens out there waiting to be discovered. Another year or two without results threatened to lead donors to believe that investing their millions in search of new dinosaur discoveries was a fool's errand.

With each day that passed, Osborn felt his place slipping further in the hierarchy of the museum. What was worse, there was little promise that things would turn around soon. It would still be at least a year or two before the *Diplodocus* fossil discovered by Brown would be mounted for exhibit, and he had nothing to fill the gap. It was clear that Wieland was not the answer he had been looking for. To replace him, Osborn turned to William Reed, who remained a one-man marketplace for fossils after his deteriorating relationship with Holland led him to quit the Carnegie Museum. Osborn wrote to Wieland to inform him that his ill-fated Wyoming expedition was over.

He also ordered Granger to leave Devils Tower and ride three hundred miles south to Como Bluff to inspect Reed's quarry and report back on its possible worth. A few weeks later, Granger wrote with word that the site contained "first class" bones of an *Allosaurus* and a *Stegosaurus* that were still embedded in the rock, along with a few outcroppings of indeterminate fossils that suggested others would be revealed with more effort.

Osborn soon approved $400 to buy Reed's quarry, though it did nothing to fix his wounded ego. Nothing the American Museum had found compared with the *Diplodocus* now in the possession of the Carnegie Museum. Even its scientific name, *Diplodocus carnegii,* reminded him of his failure. If Osborn could convince Hatcher to come work at the American Museum, perhaps then he would be in a position to name a new species after his uncle J. P. Morgan, presenting his benefactor with an immortal gift that no material wealth could match. But after paying Wieland's exorbitant fee, Osborn could not afford to dangle enough money in front of Hatcher to pry him away from the Carnegie.

Osborn just had to make do without Hatcher. He sent Brown on small scouting missions late in the summer to investigate some of the dozens of unsolicited tips that the museum received each year. A high school principal named Willis T. Lee wrote to tell Osborn that he knew of a Jurassic outcrop not far from his hometown of Trinidad, Colorado. Brown spent four days searching and came away with scattered bones but nothing significant enough to justify a full expedition. Though happy to at least be back in the dinosaur hunt after half a season searching for prehistoric wood, Brown yearned for a chance at finding the giant fossils that would redeem him. The *Brachiosaurus* that Riggs was still excavating for the Field Museum was in Colorado, increasing the chances that there would be other impressive finds nearby. Brown longed to explore that area rather than hunt down another dead-end report from a rancher who had likely confused a dinosaur fossil with the remains of a steer. Yet he felt he could only hint at it. "I don't know Riggs's exact locality," Brown wrote to Osborn. "It must be rich from the newspaper stories. I wish we might have a show at it."

Neither Brown nor Osborn knew at the time that the quarry, and indeed Riggs himself, would soon be available. The Field Museum was in the process of cutting its funding for dinosaur collecting in favor of geology, the preferred field of the museum's director. Riggs's dinosaur, which was the largest specimen ever found at the time, would be the last major dinosaur addition to its collection until nearly the end of the twentieth century. Paleontologists working at the museum protested the cuts to no avail.

Osborn did not bite at Brown's unspoken request to hunt for a trophy specimen of his own. Instead, he ordered Brown to remain in eastern Colorado and collect the fossils of prehistoric mammals. Brown was not in a position to argue. He soon found the skull of a three-toed precursor of modern horses known as a *Protohippus*, as well as impressive full skeletons of a prehistoric antelope and an extinct horse known as *Hypohippus*, which was distinguished by its long neck and short legs. (Both specimens remain on display in the American Museum.) At the end of August he shipped his finds to New York and began his own trip back to the East Coast.

Osborn, meanwhile, fell further into envy. It "has been a very costly season—with many disappointments," he wrote in a letter that September. If only 1902 would bring a turn in his luck.

CHAPTER ELEVEN

THE BONES OF THE KING

Osborn sat in his office looking at a 1902 calendar and wondering what the New Year would bring. He could hear the sounds of construction coming from the forest of upscale apartment buildings growing across the Upper West Side in anticipation of the completion of the subway system, two years away. Automobiles were starting to appear on the city's streets. Farther down Broadway, workers were putting the final touches on the Flatiron Building, its triangular frame prompting the photographer Alfred Stieglitz to say that "it appeared to be moving towards me like the bow of a monster ocean steamer—a picture of a new America in the making."

History felt like it was speeding up, bringing in an era when technology and science would dominate daily life. In the rush of the new century, the traditions of the past seemed to fall one by one, ushering in a time when wit and chance mattered more than connections.

While the world changed around him, Henry Osborn bet his future on building a collection of dinosaur trophies that would stand as a monument to the millionaires who funded the American Museum—and reflect some of their glories back on himself. Unless Osborn could find the sort of gigantic fossil that would draw paying crowds, the museum was on a path to a slow, stale death.

As Osborn stretched for something to prove his worth, the museum floor still had no dinosaurs. The partial *Diplodocus* that Brown had found was not ready for exhibition. Over and over his collectors would bring in something momentous, but preparing them for a lifelike display would take years. Osborn felt time ticking away with no guarantee that he would last long enough in his position to be there when the specimens were finally finished. To fill the empty exhibit halls of the American Museum, Osborn convinced the trustees to purchase Cope's wide-ranging collection of dinosaur fossils, prehistoric mammals, and plant life.

Never a warm man, Osborn turned colder as Hatcher continued to scorn his continuing advances and poured salt in the wound with frequent friendly letters giving updates on his successes at the Carnegie. As Osborn planned for the summer prospecting season, he wrote demanding letters to his stable of collectors. "I hope you will push your work this summer with great energy and persistence, and accomplish fine results," he wrote to Granger. "I have had the feeling during this last year that you have not put quite enough of this element into your work." In a letter to Brown, he subtly highlighted the fact that he had not found a significant dinosaur fossil since his first summer working with Wortman.

He decided to send Brown to Montana, a state not yet known for abundant fossil beds, on a mission for a *Triceratops*. So far, most expeditions had centered on the proven fields of Wyoming, the Dakotas, and Colorado. Osborn sent Brown to Montana instead largely because of William T. Hornaday, the founding director of what is now known as the Bronx Zoo. Hornaday had explored Montana the previous summer with a photographer to document the lives of blacktail deer in what would later be recognized as one of the first steps of the conservation movement in America. While traveling through Montana in 1901, Hornaday happened upon a friendly settler named Max Seiber, who took Hornaday to "a spot nearby where he had found the badly weathered remains of what once had been a fossil skull, as large as the skull of a half-grown elephant," Hornaday wrote. When he returned to New York, Hornaday showed the photographs of the find to Osborn and Brown, who instantly identified them as the remains of the elusive *Triceratops*. The only problem was that Hornaday could not remember where exactly Seiber lived, nor did he have any means of contacting him.

With a map of Montana and Hornaday's photographs, Brown headed west, trying to find the location of the specimen and perhaps some of his lost self-confidence at the same time. He was once again on his own and free to follow his wits. He needed them. Montana stood as the largest haystack he had yet to search for a single fossil, an expanse stretching slightly more than 147,000 square miles. He knew that the *Triceratops* skull was there somewhere and had the photographs to prove it. The hard part was retracing Hornaday's expedition with few clues to go by.

Not since Patagonia had Brown seen a place as empty as this. Montana joined the Union as the forty-first state in 1889, and when Brown reached it thirteen years later it had more livestock than people. Brown rode the train as far as Miles City, a small settlement that was the doorway to his ultimate goal: the Hell Creek Formation. These ragged red-and-gray ravines and stark Badlands stretch over portions of Montana, the Dakotas, and Wyoming and were once a coastal plain, but had dried out to become a sun-bleached wilderness. Though it had been sparsely explored by prospectors, the few relics collected from the region had proven to be of extraordinary size and quality. If Hornaday truly had come across a well-preserved *Triceratops* skull in Montana, then Hell Creek would be the most promising place to start.

Of all the inhospitable places that Brown's quest for dinosaurs had taken him, this was the most unforgiving. The afternoon sun broiled everything in sight, while a haze of gritty dust perpetually hung in the air and choked the lungs of anyone foolish enough to try to breathe without a bandanna covering their face. When it wasn't too hot and dry, it was too wet and windy. Sudden, violent thunderstorms boomed through the wide skies, unleashing a flurry of hail, tornadoes and floods that dared a person to survive. If the land didn't get you, then the animals would. Twisting, snarling ravines lurched across the Badlands, hiding black bears, bison, and rattlesnakes among outcroppings of rocks and fossils that date back more than 70 million years. In a land so barren, there was no hope of help if things went wrong.

The first known white explorers reached the region ninety-eight years before Brown. The Corps of Discovery, led by Meriwether Lewis and William Clark, stumbled into the Badlands in 1804 while following the path of the Missouri River in the hope that it would lead them to the Pacific. The place unnerved them like few others they encountered on their long journey. It felt haunted by a sense of menace that could not be explained merely by the realization that they were surrounded by untold numbers of dangerous animals. When they could take a moment away from focusing on their own survival, they could not help but notice the strange rocks in the shape of bones that were jutting out of the earth. Officially, they were on an eight-thousand-mile expedition meant to find a waterway across the country, establish trade with the indigenous inhabitants, and claim ownership over an area stretching from modern-day Louisiana to Montana, which the United States had purchased from France. Yet President Jefferson also asked them to keep their eyes out for a mastodon, an elephantlike creature that scientists now know became extinct roughly ten thousand years ago. But at that time Jefferson believed that the mastodons might have simply moved west before American colonists arrived.

Though the concept of a dinosaur did not yet exist, Lewis and Clark dutifully searched the landscape for intriguing stones or fossils and sent samples back to the White House. Somewhere between present-day Sioux City, Iowa, and Omaha, Nebraska, Lewis and Clark came across "a petrified Jawbone of a fish or some other animal," a discovery which grew more perplexing as it became clear that they were not near an ocean. Indeed, they noticed that the more desolate the region, the more likely it was to contain the bones of what looked to be aquatic life. In present-day South Dakota, they discovered the ribs, teeth, and backbone of a creature that stretched forty-five feet long. They deemed it a large fish, but scientists now believe that the specimen was likely the remains of a plesiosaur, a marine reptile that lived alongside dinosaurs in the Mesozoic era.

The Corps of Discovery were likely the first white explorers to find dinosaur fossils in the western half of the United States, though they did not know it. On their way back from the Pacific, they stopped at a 150-foot-tall block of rock they named Pompey's Tower—now known as Pompey's Pillar—in honor of the eighteen-month-old son of Sacagawea, a Lemhi Shoshone woman who acted as a guide and interpreter for the corps as it traveled across the continent. While there, Clark noted in a journal entry full of creative spellings that "pieces of the rib of a fish which was Semented within the face of the rock this rib is about 3 inchs in Secumpherance about the middle. . . . I have Several peces of this rib the bone is neither decayed nor petrified but very rotten. The part which I could not get out may be Seen, it is about 6 or 7 Miles below Pompey's Tower . . . about 20 feet above the water." Perhaps with the memory of a whale carcass he had viewed on the Pacific Coast, Clark reasoned that the bones were those of a similar sea creature worn away over the centuries. Modern-day paleontologists believe that he was describing a *Hadrosaurus*, a duckbilled dinosaur that is among the more common specimens in the area.

By the time Brown reached the Hell Creek region of Montana nine decades later, dinosaur fossils were something that Western ranchers were familiar with. Within a matter of weeks Brown managed to find the spot where Hornaday had snapped pictures of what appeared to be a *Triceratops* skull. Upon close inspection of the bones, however, he realized that it was not a *Triceratops* at all but the broken remains of a mosasaur—a giant predatory marine reptile. Brown resolved to stay in Hell Creek until he found something that would ensure his future with the museum. He bought three horses, a wagon full of equipment, and enough food to feed a small expedition party. He was soon joined by Richard Swann Lull, a doctoral student at Columbia University, and a young volunteer named Philip Brooks.

Tall, athletic, and pompous, Lull was six years older than Brown and outranked him in terms of academic achievement. Yet Brown had more field experience and knew how to survive in the harshest conditions. Still, it was Brown's first time heading a group expedition for the museum, and even little things tripped him up. There was so much to do, and so much that could go wrong—not only for him but for the museum, which desperately needed some good news from the field.

In early July, Brown's party arrived in the hamlet of Jordan, a hundred miles northwest of Miles City. Founded three years earlier, Jordan was a lawless, isolated, and dangerous place with the grim distinction of being located farther from a railroad station than any other settlement in the country. Brown led the expedition team to the banks of Hell Creek, where they made camp. He took a horse and went on solitary scouting trips through the ravines and foothills. Brown had a talent for surviving in nearly any conditions, but was still taken aback by the difficulty of the terrain.

Even in one of the most hostile places on Earth, the demands of New York found a way to reach him. A letter from Osborn arrived on July 25, criticizing him for the wasted freight charges and labor after a shipment of fossils he had collected earlier that summer arrived at the American Museum in a broken heap due to the rough transport. Osborn wrote, "I know you sent the specimen to us after the best possible methods; but it should have received a more careful examination."

As the last days of July ticked away, Brown found himself

torn. The party uncovered a *Triceratops* skull that was in decent condition, though its horns were missing. With enough work, it could be "a fine exhibition specimen," he wrote to Osborn, knowing that would begin to make up for the crushed fossil now sitting in the museum in New York. If anything, the skull would buy him at least one more year of employment. But he wanted more. Brown felt compelled to brave another ravine, search another hillside, climb over the side of another cliff if doing so meant that he would come closer to a specimen that would put his life back on its upward track.

As July faded into August, Brown used a plow and scraper to attack a sandstone hill he called Sheba Mountain. Once Brown began to dig, however, the rock proved impervious to any blade. He sent an assistant to Miles City for dynamite to blow off all the hillside above what he hoped would be the bone layer. Brown was not in the habit of blasting away at every spot that gave him trouble, but this time he had to know what secret the Earth was protecting with such ferocity. He laid the explosives, set the timer, and waited. The blast echoed among the ravines of the Badlands. Once the smoke cleared, he stared into the deep hole he had created. It was nothing less than a time machine, bridging the 60-million-year gap between the age of the dinosaurs and our own. As he looked down into the pit, Brown took in a shape that no human being had ever laid eyes on. Brown wrote in a letter that evening to Osborn, "I have never seen anything like it."

It was as if a child's conception of a monster had become real and was laid down in stone. Though most of its skull and tail were missing, everything about the beast seemed designed to overwhelm the human mind. Its hips, nearly thirteen feet above the ground, would later be found to power legs that ran at speeds greater than ten miles per hour. Its immense jaw measured over four feet in length and could exert as much pressure as the weight of three modern cars, instantly exploding the bones of its prey. Its serrated teeth, the longest of any known dinosaur, could dig through the thick skin of a *Triceratops* and rip out five hundred pounds of flesh in one bite. In time, the creature would become perhaps the most recognizable animal the world has ever seen, its deadly silhouette and Latin name familiar even to those with no interest in dinosaurs or science. Yet in that moment in the hot August sun, the animal that would soon take the name of *Tyrannosaurus rex* was entirely new—an unmistakable set of clues that the history of life was more varied and surreal than anyone had imagined.

Brown knew that he was suddenly in a race against time. He had found the only specimen of a creature previously unknown to science, and there was no telling if he or anyone else would ever find another. Brown scrambled to uncover as much of the fossil as possible. A September snowstorm was not out of the question, which could mean that the dinosaur might have to be abandoned until spring. During that time someone from Jordan could find it and try to sell it themselves, or even destroy it through carelessness.

Brown rode his men hard. The small general store in Jordan soon ran out of lumber and plaster, the two supplies most essential in extracting a gigantic fossil out of the ground without damaging it. With no other choice, Brown turned to dynamite, taking the risk that he would not accidentally blow up the fossil before he could share it with the world. Each day, more of the animal was revealed, like the wrapping paper of a gift being removed inch by inch.

Finally, in October, Brown pulled the last section of the skeleton free. The small team of horses strained under the load, pulling the haul to Miles City in shifts. They eventually moved more than fifteen thousand pounds of bones to a boxcar that Osborn had arranged for them. As the first snow of winter fell, Brown watched as nineteen crates of fossils were loaded into the boxcar, a collection that included not only the new carnivorous dinosaur but also the skeletons of a crocodile-like *Champsosaurus* and a *Triceratops*—both of which still stand on the floor of the American Museum.

Though he knew that its contents were priceless, Brown did not accompany the train east. A prospector at heart, he could not leave Montana without poking his head around for at least a few days more. He soon walked into the lobby of the Billings State Bank on a small errand and, while waiting in line, noticed a display case containing the oversized limb bone of a dinosaur. The bank's manager revealed where the fossil had come from, and Brown spent the final days of the year camped on the banks of Beaver Creek searching for the remainder of the specimen.

When the train carrying the crates reached New York, what would become the most famous dinosaur in the world looked no different from every other fossil Brown had found, encased in a cocoon of white plaster with the letters *AMNH* painted in black on its side. It would be two years before museum technicians fully cleaned and prepared the skeleton of the *T. rex*. Until then, Osborn still thought he was losing the fossil race. "I think we have the finest carnivorous Dinosaur material in the world; but I envy the Carnegie Museum their complete skeletons. We are certainly not holding our own . . . both Carnegie and Chicago have done better than we have," he wrote in a letter at the end of the prospecting season.

NEW BEGINNINGS

Nothing about the creature made sense.

In a laboratory high above the American Museum's exhibition halls, Lull directed a team of preparators as they cut open the plaster jacket holding the bones of the newly discovered dinosaur. They began chipping and chiseling at the stone, taking care not to let their impatience get the better of them. In the field, the work of a paleontologist was all action, locked in a battle with the elements to free a specimen from the earth before it crumbled. In the laboratory, the work was painful and slow, requiring delicacy above all.

A collector had to trust that another dinosaur fossil always lay around the bend. A preparator never forgot how close they were to disaster. Every action was a hypothesis put to an instant test. One wrong choice—pressing too hard, sanding too closely, brushing too vigorously—and a bone more than 60 million years old could be shattered, destroying priceless evidence of Earth's history that might never be found again. Once all traces of rock and dust were finally cleared from a section of bone, it was coated in layers of shellac to prevent it from crumbling. Work then turned to the next bone segment, rebuilding the puzzle of life piece by painful piece.

Over the course of two years, Brown's discovery began to take shape. Osborn watched as the creature's jaw, vertebrae, ribs, shoulder, and pelvic bones emerged from a bed of rock, all the while imagining how they fit into a living, breathing animal. The questions the specimen posed came faster than any answers. First among them, why did an immense creature have such strangely small and seemingly useless forelimbs? Nothing as diminutive had been found in the fossil record among carnivorous dinosaurs, nor in any of their prey. The forelimbs were not the only puzzling aspect of the beast's bones. Upon inspecting them, Osborn realized that the bones of its hind limbs were hollow, like those of a bird, making the creature the most prominent example of how prehistoric life blurred the lines of the animal kingdom.

Some forty years before Brown's discovery, workers at a limestone quarry in Solnhofen, Germany, unearthed a nearly complete fossil marked by clear impressions of spread wings and tail feathers etched in the stone. Its anatomy suggested two creatures at once. The feathers and the air sacs in its backbone indicated a prehistoric bird. The body—including developed teeth, a long tail, and three clawed fingers capable of independent movement (unlike the fused fingers of living birds)—pointed toward a reptile. A local natural history professor determined in 1861 that it was a reptile. The British Museum of Natural History soon purchased the find, and Richard Owen decided to reclassify it as a bird with the name *Archaeopteryx macrura.*

This decision all but ignored the evidence that the specimen was just the sort of transitional fossil between two species that Darwin had theorized in the *Origin of Species* but had yet to be found in the fossil record. Darwin wondered, "Has God demented Owen, as a punishment for his crimes, that he should overlook such a point?" Darwin cited the fossil—which became known as the "London specimen"—in updated editions of his landmark book as an example showing that life does not have fixed categories. "Hardly any recent discovery shows more forcibly than this, how little we as yet know of the former inhabitants of the world," he wrote. At roughly 160 million years old, *Archaeopteryx* is now considered one of the earliest known birds. Studies of its DNA show that it was covered in jet-black feathers, like a raven. Nor was it the only bird living alongside dinosaurs. In 2005, paleontologists in Antarctica discovered a 68-million-year-old creature known as *Vegavis iaai*, which looked remarkably like a modern duck, suggesting that other birds were there in some form all along.

A small animal that combined features of reptiles and birds was one thing. Discovering a massive carnivorous dinosaur with birdlike body architecture was quite another. As he studied Brown's specimen in front of him, Osborn slowly began to realize it was a scientific marvel in every sense, unlocking a door to a distant Earth that had been closed for 60 million years. The existence of such a large predator implied there had been a complex ecosystem far removed from the land of fat, lazy giants that Owen had imagined.

Gigantic herbivores were well known at this point, which meant there had been a lush prehistoric environment that provided enough plant life to sustain them. A carnivore of the same immense size, on the other hand, suggested that animal life must have been more plentiful than previously imagined.

Otherwise, how could an enormous predator find enough food to survive? And if life was more plentiful, that implied some form of social structure, suggesting that dinosaurs could have been capable of moving in herds, like land-bound flocks of birds.

The questions posed by Brown's discovery came in waves. A creature this huge and ferocious had to hunt, but how? It had to roam, since otherwise it would exhaust all sources of food quickly—but how far? And if an animal like this existed, its potential prey must have developed some form of defense—but what? Nothing before had ever demonstrated the ferocity of evolution in such an obvious form. At the end of the late Jurassic period (around 145 million years ago), an extinction event erased giant sauropods like the *Brachiosaurus* from the Earth. Some 40 million years later, life had somehow found a way to reorder itself into the monster whose bones were now spread out in a Manhattan laboratory.

Its size struck Osborn for other reasons as well. Throughout his career, he had a tendency to view the history of life on Earth as a sort of morality tale in which good prevailed in the end. In that light, Brown's discovery was the perfect example that muscle alone does not guarantee survival. Its disappearance opened up the ecological space for mammals, which were blessed with greater intelligence and the capacity to care for one another. The failure of a species with a body so powerful, and the triumph of humans with bodies so weak by comparison, seemed to Osborn evidence of a great plan that peaked with present-day Anglo-Saxon humans in their rightful position of power.

Osborn had long wanted a giant that would prove his worth. Now he had the biggest meat-eater that ever lived. By 1905, he understood enough about the animal to let the world in on the secret. The first person to publish a scientific description of a newly discovered species gets the honor of naming it, following an international convention which typically uses some combination of a description of its distinctive features, where the species was found, or the person who found it. *Stegosaurus*, for instance, has its root in the Greek word for roof, inspired by Marsh's ultimately incorrect assumption that its plates lay flat on its back as a sort of protective barrier above its body. Other well-known species were named for their memorable appearance (*Triceratops*, three-horned face); the sound they likely made when they walked (*Brontosaurus*, the thunder lizard); or the simple fact that they hadn't been seen before (*Allosaurus*, the strange lizard). Hatcher, with his decision to name the *Diplodocus* specimen after Carnegie, had expanded naming possibilities to include patrons of museums, giving prehistoric bones the power to reflect a human's social worth.

Hatcher upstaged him once. Osborn was now in a position to return the favor. In a move that broke with convention and displayed an element of showmanship reminiscent of P. T. Barnum, Osborn announced that the species that Brown had unearthed would be named *Tyrannosaurus rex*, meaning tyrant lizard king. The name was lyrical and justified by the creature's outsized body and position at the top of the prehistoric food chain. But beyond the scientific reasons, Osborn would forever be linked with the one species known as a king, elevating his own place in paleontology above any competitors. With this creature, his time had finally come.

Though *T. rex* now had a name, no one outside the museum had yet seen it. In February of that year, the American Museum unveiled a seventy-foot-long *Brontosaurus* (now known as

Apatosaurus) as the centerpiece of its new Dinosaur Hall. It was the first time that a fully assembled sauropod had stood on the floor of the museum. Thousands of New Yorkers came to view the giant. The reaction of visitors once they stood in front of the bones seemed a mirror into their own lives. One boy asked an attendant if the dinosaur would eat him. A butcher calculated how many pounds of meat he could reap from the animal. A truck driver pondered aloud what kind of traction the beast's claws gave it on a slippery road. It was as if ordinary New Yorkers stumbled upon a passage into a prehistoric world, only to find themselves there. The presence of the dinosaur was like a window shade pulled open, revealing that science was not only for the privileged but something that could be as universal and understood as sunshine.

Attendance rose 25 percent that year, a considerable jump. Yet while the new dinosaur specimens brought in more visitors, few lingered in the hall. The bones of Jumbo, the circus elephant, remained the most popular exhibit. A few weeks after the *Brontosaurus* was unveiled, the usual crowds once again formed around the gem exhibits and other favorites, leaving the paleontology rooms mostly empty. Osborn could not help but notice that one impressive dinosaur was simply not enough. For paleontology to fully capture visitors' attention, the museum would have to move past displays of isolated specimens and show the vast complexity of the prehistoric world, turning dinosaurs from curiosities into passports to the past. Exhibiting a mounted *T. rex*, the fearsome predator of huge sauropods, would open a window into a dangerous world where species had to compete for survival in a primordial landscape, providing drama that could not be found in any one-off display of a P. T. Barnum–type novelty.

There was a problem, however. As the significance of the

T. rex grew, Osborn could not look past the fact that the specimen was missing too many key bones to build a realistic display. Three years after Brown discovered the first *T. rex*, Osborn sent him back into the unforgiving landscape of Hell Creek to find another one. Brown readily accepted the assignment, but he wasn't going alone.

Brown had somehow found a way to bring Marion back into his life. Even though every summer found him toiling in the sort of unforgiving places that people went out of their way to avoid, every fall he would return. And when he did, Brown made it a priority to stand outside Erasmus Hall in Brooklyn, then the city's most prestigious public high school for science, to greet Marion at the end of her days of teaching. The two spent hours walking through Brooklyn's Prospect Park, building a connection based on their shared love of the natural world. In Marion, Brown had found someone whose combination of intellect and humor allowed him to drop his defenses and ignore his instinct to roam. She, in turn, delighted in his distinctive mix of purpose and fun. Marion became the stable tether to the present that was often lacking in his profession.

On February 13, 1904—one day after Brown's thirty-first birthday—they were married at St. Paul's Episcopal Church in Marion's hometown of Oxford, New York. The day was cold and sunny. Before the ceremony, Marion wore bright-red socks over her white satin slippers to keep her feet warm. She had already started walking down the aisle when she realized she still had them on. "With a muffled giggle and two vigorous kicks, she got rid of them just in time," their daughter, Frances, later wrote.

For their honeymoon, they spent five months in the field

prospecting, finally knitting together the two sides of Brown's life. Over the following weeks, they braved every extreme the west had to offer: temperatures which climbed to 105 degrees; hailstorms accompanied by more than four inches of rain within an hour; and vast swarms of mosquitoes. As he worked to excavate a duckbill skeleton near the Judith River, she took detailed notes while watching a toad give birth to thirteen babies. "The old toad never paid the slightest attention to them after they were born," she wrote.

They took a circular route across the country. In New Mexico, Marion studied the techniques with which Navajo women wove patterned woolen blankets while Brown searched nearby rock outcrops, eventually discovering a new specimen of hadrosaur now known as *Kritosaurus navajovius*, which is currently on display in the American Museum. From there, they traveled to Arizona and then to Arkansas. One night in camp, Brown spied a copperhead snake poised to strike Marion. He whispered to her to remain perfectly still while he took out his revolver and killed it with one shot. "Decades later, Barnum remarked that Marion's instinctive reaction to his unexplained command was an example of the perfect rapport between them," their daughter later wrote.

Brown returned to the quarry near Jordan, Montana, in 1905, with Marion at his side. He didn't bring her presence to Osborn's attention, because to him, Marion had become another part of himself, as inseparable from his body as his nose. In the three years since Brown's discovery of the *T. rex*, what was once a dangerous and isolated place had become a regular stop on the summer prospecting circuit. Thanks to dinosaurs, Jordan had evolved into the mania of a gold-rush town, a mixture equal parts desperation and greed.

Brown learned that a crew from the Carnegie Museum had swept through a few weeks before without finding any worthy specimens, though they had respected the custom among collectors and left his previous quarry alone. No one but Brown had ever found a *T. rex*, leaving open the question of whether it was a feat that could be repeated. Hoping that his luck would not run out, Brown and his expedition soon located the quarry and began blasting away at the rocks he had used to seal it and building new earthworks to support further excavation. He found something almost immediately.

Less than six feet away from the location of the specimen he had discovered in 1902, Brown uncovered a *T. rex* skull that when pulled from the stone weighed more than eight hundred pounds. The job of fully extracting it, however, proved to be one of the greatest physical challenges Brown ever faced. One block of stone containing bones from the specimen weighed 4,150 pounds and required six horses to pull it out of the quarry. Round after round of blasting and scraping expanded the pit to one hundred feet long, twenty feet deep, and fifteen feet wide, by far the biggest that Brown ever made.

As he dug deeper, Brown kept careful note of the rock layers he unveiled. Near the end of the season he felt confident enough to share with Osborn a theory that he had been formulating for several years. "I am fully convinced after several years of work that the [coal-bearing] beds are separate and distinct from the [dinosaur-bearing beds]. I have yet to find a dinosaur bone in the [coal-bearing beds]," he wrote.

Over the next two years he continued to refine his thoughts and eventually wrote and published one of his rare scientific articles. In the paper, he described how, over time, the rock layers that caught his eye would be found to have high levels of iridium, an extremely dense metal that is rare on Earth but unusually abundant on asteroids and comets. The presence of such material from a likely interstellar source is now seen as powerful evidence for the theory that a large asteroid or comet played a key role in the extinction of dinosaurs by drastically altering the Earth's climate.

In early August, Osborn surprised Brown with word that he planned to travel to Jordan to oversee the last stages of the dig. Only then did Brown confess that Marion had been at his side the whole summer. "Mrs. Brown did accompany me from my home to camp and had done the cooking for the outfit this summer reducing our living expenses about half," Brown wrote, hoping to appeal to Osborn's sense of thrift. "I did not discuss the matter with you for it seemed a purely personal matter with me as long as I performed my duty without any added expense on her account and the Museum has certainly been the gainer."

Osborn ultimately did not go to Montana that summer and made no mention of Marion's presence on the expedition team. The relationship between the two men had changed. Brown now had the distinction of having discovered the world's most fearsome carnivore—an achievement that would be sure to draw the attention of the Carnegie or any other institution that wanted to rival the American Museum. For the first time in his career, Osborn was forced to treat Brown with a light touch. Though his own profile had risen thanks to his association with the *T. rex*, Osborn still needed Brown—and his ability to find impressive

Brown holds the reins as a team of horses hauls *T. Rex* fossils weighing over 4,100 pounds out of a quarry in Hell Creek, Montana, in 1905. Brown discovered the first *T. rex* specimen in the same quarry three years earlier.

specimens—as a bridge to becoming the king he envisioned himself to be.

After all, the world's most famous dinosaur at the time was not the tyrant lizard king but the specimen about to pass into the hands of the king of the British Empire. In 1902, King Edward VII visited Andrew Carnegie in his castle in Scotland and, upon seeing a sketch of the skeleton of a *Diplodocus* hanging on the wall, asked what it could possibly be. "The hugest quadruped that ever walked the Earth, a namesake of mine," Carnegie replied. Unfamiliar with the difficulty of finding a complete set of fossils, the king asked if Carnegie had a similar specimen that he could spare. Carnegie offered a plaster copy, and in early 1905 thirty-six boxes containing 292 replica bones arrived in London. (The original bones remained in Pittsburgh, and would not be ready for display until 1907.)

Carnegie was one of the first to grasp the true power that gigantic dinosaurs had to create a sense of unity through humanity's shared appreciation of the size and mystery of these extinct beasts. He believed the great cost and labor put into the dinosaur replica was worthwhile because through it "an alliance for peace was forged between England and America." This gift was the beginning of what became known as Carnegie's dinosaur diplomacy. He soon gave additional replicas of the *Diplodocus* to museums throughout Europe in the belief that forging cultural bonds between countries would prevent future wars. The London specimen, now known as Dippy, became a national phenomenon, packing visitors into the National History Museum in record numbers.

Osborn had nothing that captured such worldwide attention. As the 1905 field season drew to a close, he pinned his hopes on the future success of the *T. rex*, hoping that the monster he held in storage would vault him—and the institution—past his rivals.

CHAPTER THIRTEEN

THE HARDEST WORK HE COULD FIND

N ew York in 1906 was a city bursting with diversions. At the Polo Grounds, the New York Giants drew nearly half a million people to watch a baseball season spent in the distant wake of the first-place Chicago Cubs. For those looking for indoor forms of entertainment, the Metropolitan Museum of Art that year brought in just under 800,000 visitors.

Getting tourists to actually come through the doors of any museum was becoming more of a challenge. An entrepreneur from Colorado named Henry J. Mayham had purchased a multilevel, open-topped motorized bus featuring a roving tour guide who used a megaphone to shout out factoids of history along a twelve-mile route.

Not that you needed to go out into the streets for excitement. Millions of New Yorkers grabbed their newspapers each day to read the latest in a murder "trial of the century" gripping the country. Harry Thaw, a Pittsburgh millionaire, had shot and killed star architect Stanford White as he sat watching a musical in Madison Square Garden (a building White had designed).

In such a cityscape, it was hard for anything—even a forty-foot-long *Brontosaurus*—to stand out. Daily visitor tallies at the

American Museum of Natural History were down nearly 15 percent from the year before. Osborn had been promoted to president of the museum, putting the full weight of the institution's future on his shoulders. Though it was a scientific marvel, the disappointing attendance for the *Brontosaurus* exhibit made Osborn's hopes that mounted dinosaur displays would make the museum a top destination look increasingly foolish.

In a final effort to put a good face on a bad year, he unveiled an exhibit featuring the feet, legs, and lower pelvis of the *Tyrannosaurus rex* on December 29, 1906. It was the first time any portion of the creature had been put on public display, and broke with Osborn's reluctance to display any dinosaur before the full mount was ready. Yet he felt boxed into a corner. He desperately needed some good press for the museum, if only to convince donors that their money was not wasted.

A few days before the exhibit opened, the *New York Times* described the *T. rex* as "The Prize Fighter of Antiquity Discovered and Restored" in an article that incorrectly bolstered Osborn's role in finding the specimen. "Of the tyrannosaurus, the greatest of flesh-eating animals, the only known specimen is the one discovered in Montana by Prof. Henry F. Osborn, and now mounted and placed on exhibition for the first time in the Natural History Museum," the paper reported. A photo that ran alongside the piece showed a museum worker whose height reached slightly below the creature's knees, dusting its pelvis with a broom.

In the frenzy to share the species with the world, Osborn neglected a fact that had been obvious since the first dinosaur fossils were put on public display. Visitors might be awed by the size of an animal's limbs, but what they really want to see is its head. In time, the skull of the *T. rex*—with its oversized nostrils, imposing size, and sinister jaws and teeth—would become one of the most recognizable silhouettes in all of science. But at that moment Osborn had nothing to show.

Osborn's usual solution to any problem was to send Brown into the wilderness and expect him to come back with something important to live up to his nickname "Mr. Bones." Yet for the first time in nearly a decade, that option was unavailable because Brown needed to remain in Brooklyn with Marion, who was pregnant with their first child. He was at her side when their daughter, Frances, was born on January 2, 1908.

The long break from digging finally gave Brown his first opportunity to focus on the academic side of paleontology. He spent months working out the details of how to mount the museum's collection of *Anatosaurus* specimens—large duckbilled dinosaurs that lived in North America roughly 65 million years ago. He also wrote some of the few professional papers he published in his lifetime.

Though he tried, Brown was not built to stay in one place for long. Becoming a father did little to quiet the inner voice that always told him to seek out new places. With Marion's blessing, he began planning an expedition to the Big Dry region of Montana, about thirty miles east of the Hell Creek beds where he discovered the first *T. rex*. The sediment formations were similar, increasing the chances that another important specimen could be found.

Brown left New York in early June with a renewed appreciation of the freedom and possibilities of the open west. He seemed to have an innate feel for the land, reading the rocks and pushing past the physical constraints of others in ways that he could not teach. But getting to that point—knowing where to dig a new quarry, or how to have the luck to find a dinosaur fossil jutting out of the ground—was often a result of his mastery of the softer science of friendship. With his deadpan wit and willingness to try anything at least once, Brown just knew how to get people to like him. In the lonesome communities that bordered the Badlands, friendly conversations would often lead to invitations to come out and inspect a strange bone that happened to be sitting on a rancher's land. What to an outsider seemed like a charmed life of continuous discovery was the result of Brown's intellect and drive, and the joy he took in being at the center of any party. The results of this two-pronged life in the field often made it seem like Brown had a touch of magic and was fated to find fossils where others were cursed to come home empty-handed. "Found *Tyrannosaurus* lower jaw and back of skull near one of the buttes. Will take it," Brown wrote in his journal in early July.

Not long after, he found fifteen connected tail vertebrae from an animal he could not immediately identify. The layers of sediment were relatively soft compared to the conditions in nearby Hell Creek, making it possible for him to dig an additional six feet into the rock without needing to turn to dynamite. The line of bones continued, suggesting the presence of a complete skeleton. He borrowed a plow from a local rancher to remove layers of topsoil and rock, and, over the following two weeks, he and an assistant chiseled the bones free. Finally, on July 15, he wrote to Osborn with news of another discovery. "Our new animal turns out to be a *Tyrannosaurus*," he wrote. "The bones are in a good state of preservation."

The new specimen was more complete than any that Brown had yet found, and included the most elusive prize: a perfectly preserved skull. For the first time, human eyes took in the complete four-foot-long head of a *T. rex*, seeing in one glance the violence that it was once capable of. Osborn immediately made plans to travel west, to see the dig that he knew would change paleontology—and his career—forever. "Your letter of July 15, makes me feel like a prophet and the son of a prophet, as I felt that you would surely find a *Tyrannosaurus* this season," he wrote. "I congratulate you with all my heart on this splendid discovery. . . ."

Osborn arrived on August 26 and attention immediately turned to the question of how to get the bones back to New York safely—not an easy task when just the lower jaw of the creature weighed about 1,000 pounds. Brown insisted on loading the full specimen onto one train rather than parceling it out into several shipments to save on costs. Osborn supported this decision, leaving Brown in a race against the coming winter. Snow started falling in late September, well before he was finished. Still he worked, dragging and digging and dynamiting until he pulled each section of fossil from the rock. The loads were so heavy that wagons kept breaking down under their weight. In the end, it took sixteen horses to pull five loads of fossils forty-five miles to the nearest rail depot, finally bringing the full splendor of the *T. rex* out of the dusty pockets of the Badlands and into the modern world.

The *T. rex* was a revolutionary find, and Osborn felt an obligation to do it justice. He knew the public was more drawn to spectacle than to science. The *T. rex* exhibit had the power to make the real science into a captivating spectacle.

Brown (right) helps hoist the pelvis of a *T. rex* specimen he discovered in Montana into a crate to ship to the American Museum in 1908. The fossils are covered in plaster to protect them until they reach the museum, where the years-long process of mounting them onto an armature would begin.

Osborn wanted to convey a sense of movement and danger, making visitors feel that they were stepping onto a planet that looked very different from their own. That subtly implied that their world might also look very different tomorrow. He asked an artist working in the paleontology department to sculpt a scale model of the animal's full skeleton, and then asked several designers to submit their best ideas.

Eventually, Osborn chose a display suggested by Raymond Ditmars, who had helped found the Bronx Zoo's popular reptile house. Ditmars proposed a scene in which a *T. rex* is in the middle of devouring a duck-billed herbivore when another *T. rex* attempts to steal its meal. "The crouching figure reluctantly stops eating and accepts the challenge, partly rising to spring on its adversary," Brown wrote, describing the planned exhibition design. The size of the exhibition hall would ultimately prove too small to contain Ditmars's proposed mount, however, leaving Osborn to scale back his ambitions.

Over the course of his career, Brown discovered dozens of species and rarely concerned himself with how their final displays would appear. Yet the *T. rex* was different. In its monumental size, Brown saw a validation of his own ambitions. He had discovered a creature that would stand forever in a prominent spot in what was becoming, thanks to his efforts, one of the most important museums in the world. He had seen the world, married a woman he loved, and become a father, fulfilling all the dreams that he dared to ask of himself. And with a perfect *T. rex* skull undergoing its slow restoration process in the museum's laboratories, he knew that there were greater accolades to come.

Over the next two years, Brown's life fell into a dependable pattern: summers in the field and the rest of the year in the city, making a daily circuit between the museum and the family's Brooklyn apartment. He had successfully built a bridge into a new era, making himself relevant in a changing world in ways that his own father could not.

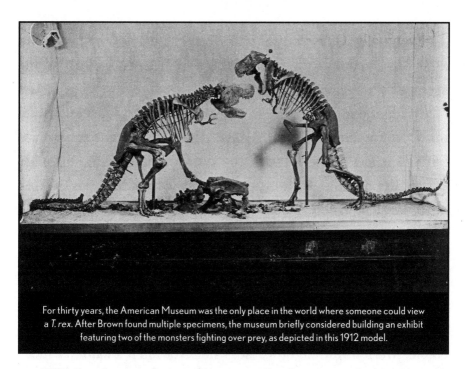

For thirty years, the American Museum was the only place in the world where someone could view a *T. rex*. After Brown found multiple specimens, the museum briefly considered building an exhibit featuring two of the monsters fighting over prey, as depicted in this 1912 model.

With its skyscrapers, subways, and palaces of culture, the New York of 1910 looked in many ways like the city of today. Yet it was a city still rooted in the past, beset by the illnesses of urban life that had plagued cities since the Middle Ages. Measles, rheumatic fever, diphtheria, and whooping cough killed thousands of New Yorkers that year. Nearly sixteen thousand newborns in 1909 did not live long enough to celebrate their first birthdays, a death toll nearly triple that of any other city in the country.

While other cities seemed to be getting healthier, New York's death rate among children under five at the start of 1910 was higher than that of London or Paris in the 1880s. Parents faced each day with fear that a wayward cough or sneeze in a crowded streetcar might unleash an invisible killer. Scarlet fever was among the city's most notorious illnesses, caused by the same bacteria that causes strep throat. Each year that a child lived seemed like another battle won. The war would continue until their fifth birthday, the age at which the diseases of urban life seemed to lose much of their lethality.

Barnum and Marion Brown celebrated when Frances turned one, thankful not only for the joy she had brought into their lives but for the fact that she had not been taken from them. At the age of two, she remained strong and healthy. On a sunny day in April 1910, Marion placed Frances in a stroller and took her on a walk in nearby Prospect Park. Though Marion would later not recall seeing anyone who was sick, Frances soon spiked a fever and broke out in a bright-red rash. Within a day, Marion developed the same symptoms. As they spiraled into sickness, Barnum did not know where to direct his fears. Each time Frances seemed stable, Marion would get worse; when Marion felt calm, Frances would appear closer to death. Antibiotics to treat scarlet fever would not be developed until 1928, nearly a full generation in the future. Instead, Barnum was left to frantically search for anyone who could help save his wife and their only child.

Frances's fever soon broke, but the family's doctors were unable to extinguish the fire that raged inside Marion's body. Brown finally asked Osborn for help, and Osborn promised he would bring in specialists from anywhere in the world at the museum's expense. But it was too late. Five days after entering Prospect Park as the healthy mother of a smiling young girl, Marion died on April 9, 1910.

With Marion's passing, Brown's tether to a normal life was slashed. The question of how to live seemed overwhelming; the duty of fatherhood simply too much. "Marion's shocked and grief-stricken parents, both then in their middle sixties, told Barnum that they would take the baby and raise her. . . . Barnum, torn with grief and anger at cruel Fate, agreed that that would be the best solution for the daughter," Frances later wrote in a memoir of her father's life.

A light went out in Barnum Brown's life. In shock, he clung to routine and formality as best as he could. "I want to thank you for the efforts to help keep my beloved wife alive, your kind letters of sympathy, and financial aid—all expressions of truest friendship for which I cannot find words to express my appreciation," he wrote in a letter to Osborn. "I shall always be deeply grateful."

Throughout his life, Brown chased the horizon to solve his problems. Less than a month after losing Marion and giving Frances to her grandparents to raise, he escaped to a hastily planned expedition into the isolated Canadian wilderness.

CHAPTER FOURTEEN

A NEW WORLD

I t was as if he wanted the elements to kill him.

The Red Deer River Valley is an isolated and unforgiving region about 130 miles east of Calgary, Canada. Gray chimneys of stone known as hoodoos soar over the rippled Badlands, which rise and fall in an unsettled rhythm. Rocky mesas give way to steep canyons that plummet as if a trapdoor had been pulled. Valleys where groves of palm trees and fir once flourished are now carved by dry riverbeds called coulees, which trace a groove below cliffs painted in bands of colors ranging from sand to copper to a gray so deep it appears purple. Aside from the shimmering water of the river, the only burst of color comes from pockets of sunflowers growing out of stone.

Only a handful of white ranchers braved this place, where in the summer great swarms of mosquitoes attacked without mercy and in the winter violent blizzards blotted out all avenues of escape. Few roads existed as late as 1910, giving the region a timeless quality that made it impossible to tell what year, or century, it was. There, in one of the most secluded spots in North America, Barnum Brown attempted to escape the weight of his pain by getting as far away from Frances and the memory of Marion as he could. He packed enough supplies to last for months and set off without much of a plan in mind. He built a flat-bottomed boat and pitched a tent on its deck, creating a mobile camp that ensured isolation. River currents took him through canyons with walls looming more than 250 feet above. The emptiness of the land was healing.

Though Osborn and Brown knew of reports that abundant fossils had been located there by a Canadian geologist in the late 1880s, the Red Deer River Valley became a point of focus only in 1909, when a rancher from the area visited the American Museum of Natural History and asked to speak with a curator. He was soon giving Brown detailed descriptions of the large fossil bones jutting out from the canyon walls on his ranch, which looked just like those in the museum halls.

Brown possessed some of the few maps in existence that marked likely fossil sites, but during those lonesome weeks on the river chance was his guide. He just let the boat ride along the current until he spotted a potential prospecting site.

The routine was soothing, a daily reminder that he had a purpose. He could not control the unseen virus that had robbed him of his wife. Nor could he face the fact that he felt unfit to take care of his young daughter. So he did the only thing he knew how to do. Brown uncovered fossils, dozens of them, all of them worthy of display. He remained in the field deep into the fall, refusing to turn back as the first week of September bombarded him with sheets of rain and sleet. "This is without doubt the richest Cretaceous deposit in America . . . with our numerous boxes on board containing such a variety of creatures we are living in a veritable ark," he wrote to Osborn.

He gave in when the full force of winter made it impossible

to continue. Over the next few months, he never stayed in one place for long. After a quick visit to the family farm in Carbondale, followed by a short trip to Oxford, New York, to see Frances, Brown raced south to Texas and then to Mexico, where he discovered fossilized mammoths. By the start of April 1911 he sailed to Cuba, where he uncovered the remains of alligators, crocodiles, turtles, and a nearly complete skeleton of a *Megalocnus*—a giant sloth that went extinct just a few thousand years ago. Soon it stood in the museum's Hall of Mammals and Their Early Relatives.

Yet wherever he traveled, Brown's thoughts kept returning to the secluded Red Deer River Valley. In mid-July he once again headed north to Alberta. There, he felt at peace for the first time since Marion's death the year before. He stayed all summer and returned the next, slowly feeling a renewed sense of daring. Soon, he was hanging off the side of a bluff, dangling by a rope as he chiseled away at rocks that he hoped contained fossils. A few weeks later, he led a field crew farther down the river, their bodies completely covered by thick clothing despite the broiling heat. "I cannot approximate the number of mosquitoes," Brown wrote, "but every person who moves about is forced to wear a net over the face, gloves, and a coat or extra heavy shirt. I have never experienced anything like it."

As details of Brown's finds leaked out, Canadian newspapers and scientists started to ask why an American was allowed to take some of the country's greatest treasures to New York without paying for them. In response, the Geological Survey of Canada asked Charles H. Sternberg and his three sons to collect specimens that would remain in Canadian hands.

Sternberg had turned a season of collecting for Cope while

studying at Kansas State University into a career as a freelance collector, eventually selling dinosaur specimens to major museums ranging from San Diego to Sweden, as well as the American Museum in New York. Brown learned of Sternberg's plan to prospect through the Red Deer River Valley in the summer of 1912 through his son, George, who was working with the American Museum that summer. The appearance of another prospecting party in a region to which Brown retreated for solace seemed to spark his sense of competition.

In early September, with only a few weeks remaining in the collecting season, Brown set off in a motorboat 150 miles downstream to reach a rock outcropping that he had noticed the year before while on a surveying mission. There he found and began excavating the nearly complete skeleton of a previously unknown duckbilled herbivore with a crescent-shaped helmet

Brown was one of the first paleontologists to uncover gigantic dinosaur fossils in Canada. Here, he stands next to his find of a *Corythosaurus*—a duck-billed herbivore—in Alberta in 1912.

Fossils that are uncovered rarely come out in one piece. Here, Brown and a team of assistants work to put together all the fragments of a *Hoplitosaurus*, which was known for its armor-like scales that ran along its back.

on its skull. Brown dubbed it *Corythosaurus*, meaning Corinthian helmet lizard, yet he was struck by something else about the specimen. Its underside was covered in skin impressions, making it appear more like a mummy than a collection of bones. He had never seen anything like it. Brown rushed to excavate the specimen before exposure to the sun and the weather destroyed it, and shipped it back to New York just as winter made further explorations impossible. Over three summers in the Canadian wilderness, Brown rebuilt himself, shedding his grief and replacing it with a renewed desire to explore.

When he returned to New York the packed-in city seemed overwhelming, a crush of people unimaginable when floating down a Canadian river just a few weeks earlier. Brown spent his first days back in the city inside the museum, briefing Osborn on what he had found, checking on the progress of the mounts of his discoveries from past seasons in the field, and walking the exhibition floors to see what drew the largest crowds. There were finally crowds, thanks to Osborn's efforts to bring in more tours of schoolchildren in hopes that they would return with their parents in tow. The museum's attendance jumped 17 percent over the previous year, edging closer to the 1-million-annual-visitors mark.

Dinosaurs grew more popular every year. The wing holding the partial *T. rex* exhibit was now among the most visited in the museum, drawing attention away from the bones of Jumbo the elephant, which had delighted a generation of children before. Brown had spent his life trying to fill the halls of the museum. That work had changed the world, making it seem entirely

Dinosaur fossils were not the only thing that Brown discovered. Over the course of his career, he uncovered prehistoric horses, mammals, fish, and a giant land tortoise like this specimen that is now in the Hall of Vertebrate Origins.

natural that extinct monsters would be displayed for any child who wished to see them.

The inclusion of dinosaurs into everyday life was a phenomenon that went beyond the halls of the American Museum. Dinosaurs were starting to represent tangible, undeniable evidence of a path of evolution which had its endpoint in Anglo-Saxon civilization, reflecting a widespread belief that race was closely linked to intelligence and ability. While we now know this to be false, this malicious line of thought ran through the American Museum in displays ranging from African artifacts to a diorama depicting the first encounters between English settlers and Native Americans in New York. Osborn installed exhibits that implied an upward ascent of evolution ending in what he called the Nordic race. The Hall of the Age of Man, for instance, began with the displays of the ancient peoples of Africa before moving to the tribes of North America and ending with Europe, suggesting a ladder in which light-skinned humans were the product of billions of years of refinement.

The twin fields of natural history and conservation were filled with men who saw no separation between their beliefs in science and in racial hierarchy. The endpoint of this line of thought was the eugenics movement, which wrongly claimed that applying the principles of genetic selection to the human population would cure the Earth of "undesirables," ranging from the physically ill to darker-skinned peoples. Madison Grant, who helped found the Bronx Zoo and created the first organizations dedicated to protecting the California redwoods and American bison, argued that humans had now replaced natural selection, having "complete mastery of the globe" and "the responsibility of saying what forms of life shall be preserved." In 1916, Grant would write *The Passing of the Great Race, or The Racial Basis of European History,* in which he argued that noble Nordic instincts and talent for self-governance were being diluted by the growing numbers of southern European immigrants whom he found undesirable. Osborn wrote a foreword for the book praising Grant's theories. Adolf Hitler wrote a letter to Grant calling the book "my bible."

The magnificent dinosaurs in the American Museum's collection provided Osborn with an irresistible lure. Visitors interested in the spectacle of prehistoric monsters had to walk through exhibit halls which implied that a racial hierarchy was as natural and correct as the positions of the bones mounted on each armature. This allowed Osborn's toxic racial influence to grow as dinosaurs expanded into popular culture.

Osborn's insistence on racial hierarchy led to his shameful decision in 1921 to offer the American Museum's Hall of Man as the venue for the Second International Eugenics Congress. Researchers from Europe and North America gathered to discuss how to maintain "virtuous" genetic traits in a world in which global cultures were mingling and mixing. The event brought together well-known scientists from around the world, including Alexander Graham Bell, the inventor of the telephone, and Leonard Darwin, the fourth son of Charles Darwin and a former member of Parliament. Through eugenics, Leonard Darwin said, "the end of our species may be long postponed and the race be brought to higher levels of racial health, happiness, and effectiveness." Osborn understood that the rising influence and popularity of the American Museum gave his destructive theories of racial superiority greater scientific weight.

The growing popularity of dinosaurs made the museum's early struggles for relevance and funding seem like a dim memory. Brown often found himself besieged by questions from movie studios and authors. He welcomed every escape from the city on an expedition where his concerns were narrowed down to finding the next fossil. At the age of forty, he was no longer a young man. Yet he had none of the ties and responsibilities of adulthood. His only immediate family was a daughter he rarely saw. His home was as much the road as it was the small apartment he kept in Brooklyn.

Brown spent the summer of 1913 competing with the Sternbergs in the Red Deer River Valley, once again hiding from the modern world in pursuit of buried monsters. His 1913 season was a disappointment by his standards, especially when the Sternbergs began to find impressive specimens. He began the 1914 season in the Canadian outback alarmed at the continued success of his competitors.

The field was often his fortress, but in the summer of 1914 Brown could no longer hide. In early July, a letter from Osborn informed him that "the great European war has just burst . . . I can only hope it will not involve the finances of the Museum in any way." Later that summer, he received another letter from the museum that warned him of the changed world he would return to. "The war is going to be a long and exhausting struggle, and the longer it lasts the harder we shall be hit by it," it read.

CHAPTER FIFTEEN

THE MONSTER UNVEILED

I n October 1915, poorly prepared British forces fired cylinders of chlorine gas at German trenches dug into the marshy meadows in northern France, the first time that the British Army used chemical warfare. Still, the British suffered over fifty thousand casualties that month, nearly double that of the Germans.

That same month, a poet named Sara Bard Field led rallies for women's suffrage as she drove cross-country from San Francisco to Washington, D.C., to deliver a petition to President Woodrow Wilson demanding a constitutional amendment granting women the right to vote. She eventually reached the White House in early January, armed with more than half a million signatures and the popular slogan "No Votes, No Babies!"

Along the eastern seaboard, the Boston Red Sox defeated the Philadelphia Phillies in five games to win the World Series, an ending so quick that a young Boston pitcher by the name of Babe Ruth made only one appearance during the entire match-up.

And at the corner of Seventy-Seventh Street and Central Park West, the world got its first glimpse of a fully mounted *Tyrannosaurus rex*. There in the center of the Hall of the Age of Man, stood a beast eighteen and a half feet tall that looked capable of stepping off its pedestal at any moment and leaving a trail of destruction across Manhattan.

Until that time, nearly every impressive dinosaur specimen in a museum exhibit anywhere in the world had been an herbivore, giving the impression that dinosaurs were outsized reptilian cows. That belief fell away in the presence of a massive carnivore, as if a sheet had finally been pulled down, revealing a world that had been hidden from view. Predation, protection, competition, decay: each aspect of the great struggle of life came together in the presence of a creature whose obvious power implied a full and vibrant ecosystem. The *T. rex*'s dominance needed no scientific explanation to be understood. Its strength was undeniable, forcing the realization that even the most powerful life form's stay on Earth was not permanent. Physically, the beasts were monsters. Symbolically, they implied that humans, too, would one day be replaced.

In truth, the *T. rex* on display was not the remains of one animal but several. With the only three known skeletons of *T. rex* in his possession, Osborn directed his staff to choose the best parts of each, combining bones to create a display that was both the remnants of once-living creatures and a sculpture built with human hands. Bits of sandstone harder than granite still clung to parts of the skulls and vertebrae, a reminder of the nearly ten years of grueling work that it took to fully free the fossils from stone.

When completed, the specimen stood erect with its backbone almost vertical, like a kangaroo. Its tail dragged far behind, like the train of a wedding dress. The posture, which museum curators later dubbed a "Godzilla pose," made the beast seem

Scientists originally believed that *T. Rex* stood upright with its tail dragging behind it like a kangaroo.

even more overwhelming than its massive jaws suggested, a staggering machine of destruction. (The specimen's positioning would eventually be changed in the 1990s to reflect the fact that its backbone likely stretched out horizontally, with its tail gliding behind it in the air.) Its serrated teeth, each the size of a banana, glistened in the lamplight of the museum hall.

Osborn could not contain his sense of triumph. "This skeleton is the finest single exhibit in the department . . . and the scientific value and popular interest are enhanced by the extreme rarity of these skeletons, their gigantic size and the fierce and predatory character of the animal," he boasted in that year's annual report.

Thousands of visitors stood outside the museum each day waiting to view the beast. When it was their turn to marvel at

The *T. rex*, depicted here in its original "Godzilla pose" in 1960. In the early 1990s, staff at the museum repositioned the specimen in accordance with an updated scientific understanding so that its tail lifts off the ground and its head juts forward as if stalking prey.

the completed mount, many stepped back in fright from the shock of staring up at a towering carnivore. Newspapers across the country covered the reappearance of the long-dead monster in breathless tones. The *New York Herald* devoted a full page of photographs to the new exhibit. "Behold the tyrano as he must have looked in life," it noted. "Books tell us that the carnivorous dinosaurus tyrranosaurus [*sic*] was a flesh-eating reptile with the tendencies of a tyrant. You better believe it."

The bones themselves were just part of what made the exhibit so captivating. Next to the specimen itself hung an oil painting by a museum staffer named Charles R. Knight that would become one of the most influential artworks in the museum's history. Though he never went on a fossil expedition and had not trained as a scientist, Knight revolutionized the public conception of dinosaurs through beautiful paintings that portrayed alert, vibrant animals in moments of high danger: creeping up on an enemy, leaping with their claws out to slash an opponent in battle, or devouring the meat of their prey. In time, Knight would be recognized as the pioneer of what is now known as paleoart, a genre that incorporates scientific evidence to imagine distinct moments of drama in the lives of individual dinosaurs.

For the 1915 exhibit, Knight painted a lone adult *T. rex* scanning the distance for potential prey. Its back is nearly vertical, making it appear taller than some of the nearby trees. Its eyes seem alive, its body alert. For the first time, the creature's bones disappeared behind a colorful, fully realized animal, like finally seeing a completed building after looking only at its blueprints. Through art, Knight showed the truth of a world populated with animals that were once as real as those at the nearby Central Park Zoo. Osborn had long wanted to dazzle visitors with two *T. rex* skeletons engaged in battle. With Knight's mural, he accomplished something more: viewers could walk away with the feeling that they had been transported back in time.

The combination of art and anatomy prompted a public reaction unlike anything that had accompanied the unveiling of

Charles R. Knight became one of the most influential museum artists of any era. This 1927 mural of a *Triceratops* facing off against a *T. rex* immersed the public in the prehistoric world and helped make *T. rex* the favorite villain of early Hollywood movies.

gargantuan specimens such as a *Brontosaurus* or *Diplodocus*. Instead of focusing on size alone, commentators were suddenly struck by the question of what the discovery of the *T. rex* meant for the importance of humankind in comparison. Clearly, the *T. rex* would win a contest of sheer brawn. Mammals, however, were blessed with more brains and beauty, the *Los Angeles Times* noted in an editorial that ran just a few days after the exhibit opened. "Bigness doesn't count for everything, and we have implicit faith in the law of the survival of the fittest. Animal life may be growing 'small by degrees' but it also becomes 'beautifully less.'"

The American Museum was besieged with letters and questions, asking for an explanation of how such a ferocious creature with seemingly no natural enemies could have gone extinct. In the search for answers, scientists often projected their own prejudices. "Why they disappeared I do not certainly know— probably bigness had something to do with it; probably lack of brains had more," W. D. Matthew, who followed Osborn as head of the museum's Department of Vertebrate Paleontology, wrote in the *New York Times*, in an argument that carried a twinge of the eugenic movement's obsession with intellectual ability. The *T. rex* was the rare scary thing that made a person feel better about themselves. Had it been alive, it could easily devour a person with its teeth larger than a human brain. Yet it was extinct and humans were not, a scoreboard that seemed to confirm the superiority of reason and intelligence above raw power.

In time, evidence that a meteor crashed into the Earth and rapidly changed the climate would undercut the notion that brains had anything to do with the fate of *T. rex* and other dinosaurs. (Indeed, contemporary scientists now believe that the species was roughly as intelligent as the chimpanzee.) But at that moment, the beast provided the symbol that Osborn had long been looking for to support eugenics, with its illegitimate belief that intelligence could help humankind avoid the same fate as the dinosaurs. Osborn had his monster, and the only thing left to do was stand and watch the crowds line up to gawk at it, as his poisonous influence grew more powerful by the day.

Though the world might never have known of *T. rex* if not for Barnum Brown's willingness to brave the canyons of Hell Creek, he did not linger in New York after its unveiling. Within a few months he was back in northern Montana, trying to pinpoint the exact layers of sediment above which no dinosaur fossils could be found. Time seemed to be running away from him. In a letter to Osborn, Brown confessed that a conversation with a local rancher made him feel like Rip Van Winkle. "People tell me of a 'man who years ago took out big mastodons in the breaks,'" he wrote, both amused and saddened to realize that the man they were referring to was his younger self.

No matter how much he tried, he could never quite escape the present. Every so often, he traveled up to Oxford, where he would stay "for a few hours to see his daughter and settle finances with his father-in-law," Frances later wrote. After a visit he would often flee to the field, as if trying to keep the sense of responsibility off his scent.

That avenue of avoidance would soon close. The American Museum canceled its three planned field expeditions the following year, unsure whether the United States would enter the world war. So Brown did what came naturally to a man for whom staying in one place felt like torment: he became a spy. Brown accepted a wartime role for the U.S. Treasury Department charting the world's oil reserves using the same set of skills that allowed him to read rock formations. Hunting natural resources and mineral wealth had once pushed miners in Europe deep into quarries from which they reemerged with strange bones. Now, decades later, Brown reversed that process and used his abilities honed finding fossils to help the U.S. government find new energy reserves for the war.

His secret work continued after the museum resumed funding digs, and for the remainder of his career he maintained an association with the many tentacles of the federal government. He continued to push himself past men half his age, while the friends and rivals he had worked with during the early stages of his career retired or settled into desk jobs at prominent museums.

While Brown continued to pursue adventures that took him as far as India and Burma in search of fossils, his most famous discovery took on a life of its own. In 1914, a former newspaper cartoonist named Willis O'Brien developed a method to make it look as if miniature clay sculptures were moving on film by stopping and repositioning them one frame at a time. Using this "stop motion" technique and the help of a newsreel photographer, he made a series of five-minute films for the Edison Company, honing his skills.

In 1918, O'Brien wrote to Barnum Brown asking for technical help on a movie he planned to direct called *The Ghost of Slumber Mountain*. Brown agreed to tutor O'Brien in subjects ranging from how dinosaurs likely moved their bodies to how they traveled in packs. With Brown's input, O'Brien created the most realistic dinosaurs yet displayed on film.

Advertisements plastered across the country tempted audiences to come see as "these giant monsters of the past are seen to breathe, to live again, to move and battle as they did at the dawn of life!" The film's climax featured a battle between a *T. rex* and a *Triceratops*, the first time that a *T. rex* was a screen villain. The film brought in slightly more than $1.8 million in today's dollars, a profit more than thirty-three times the cost of its production.

Barnum Brown in 1919, four years after the first full *T. rex* specimen was revealed in New York City. He often joked that he lost his hair as a young man after encountering a mountain lion in a cave in Patagonia.

That taste of success ramped up O'Brien's ambitions. Over the next seven years, he toiled away on a film adaptation of Sir Arthur Conan Doyle's novel *The Lost*

World. It was the first full-length film to pair human actors with stop-motion dinosaurs, fulfilling every child's fantasy. When the film premiered in 1925, it featured scenes so lifelike that some audience members believed the dinosaurs were real. Herds stampede; a pterodactyl strips meat from a fresh kill; a bullet wound in the flesh of an allosaur appears to gush blood. O'Brien again featured a *T. rex* as the ultimate monster, replacing the allosaur in Conan Doyle's original text. For a model, he drew from Charles Knight's painting in the American Museum. The film's *T. rex* is so fierce that it first rips off the leg of its prey and then begins eating it alive. The film's popularity made it the archetype for monster movies, with the *T. rex* as the star. In a review, the *New York Times* noted that "some of the scenes are as awesome as anything that has ever been shown in shadow form." *The Lost World* became the first commercial film to be shown as in-flight entertainment on an airplane.

Among those who watched the film was Merian C. Cooper, a former Air Force pilot who escaped from a prisoner-of-war camp and returned to civilian life with a plan to join the growing motion-picture business. While working at RKO Studios in Hollywood, he came across a soundstage featuring O'Brien's models of dinosaurs and decided to jettison a project he was working on about baboons and instead focus on an idea in which a giant ape fights a *Tyrannosaurus.* The completed film, by then known as *King Kong,* appeared in 1933 and proved a huge success, pulling in more than $1.5 million in today's dollars during its first weekend despite the ongoing Great Depression. More than six thousand moviegoers at the newly opened Radio City Music Hall could be heard yelling and whistling when Kong faces down the *T. rex* before being kidnapped and brought to New York.

Brown made his first trip to Hollywood a few years later after receiving a call from Walt Disney, who planned to follow the commercial success of Mickey Mouse and Snow White with a film that he expected to "change the history of motion pictures." He had Brown educate animators at his studio about everything associated with dinosaurs, from different geological formations to the relationships between various species to the most up-to-date theories on why and how they became extinct.

The finished product appeared in November 1940 as a segment of Disney's masterpiece *Fantasia*. As an orchestra plays Igor Stravinsky's *The Rite of Spring*, microscopic blobs split, sea creatures form, and dinosaurs appear on a rugged, unsettled planet. Suddenly, rain begins to fall and a herd of herbivores looks up to see a *T. rex* coming for them as lightning crashes behind it. It catches up to a *Stegosaurus*, which fights it off with its spiked tail until the *T. rex* bites its neck, killing it. As the *T. rex* begins to devour its prey, the swampy world of the *T. rex* is replaced by a parched land full of downed trees and mud, and then only footprints leading to fossils. The segment offered millions of children their first impression of dinosaurs, centering the action on the power of *T. rex* that still awed visitors daily at the American Museum.

Unlike anything else found in a natural history museum, the *T. rex* morphed into a staple of popular culture. In the pages of comic books Superman fought one, Wonder Woman rode one, and Batman captured a mechanical one and kept it as a souvenir in the Batcave. At the Chicago World's Fair, an animatronic *T. rex* stood in the center of an exhibit sponsored by the Sinclair Oil Company, its gleaming rows of teeth terrifying young and old alike. In whatever form it took, the instinctive fear that the creature conjured made it a magnet, holding an audience's attention long enough to build a popular acceptance of concepts ranging from geology to climate change.

Brown would often remark that nothing else he had done in life came anywhere close to its importance. His association with the species led to appearances on radio shows and television, turning him into one of the first celebrity scientists. Each week, millions heard lectures he delivered on CBS Radio, while millions more each year viewed the specimens he had uncovered, a combination which seemed to fulfill a prophecy of showmanship handed down from his namesake, P. T. Barnum.

For all of the attention the *T. rex* brought him, there was one audience whom Brown continually shut out—Frances. As a child, she often wrote to the American Museum seeking information about her father. Once, she asked for a private tour of Brown's discoveries, as if by spending time with them she could understand what was so compelling that it made him cast her aside. W. D. Matthew, the head of the Department of Vertebrate Paleontology, wrote a short note to Brown in the field whenever Frances visited the museum, each time forcing the present into the deep past.

It would take the start of the Second World War—and Brown's fears that the *T. rex* might be destroyed—to bring the two halves of his life together.

CHAPTER SIXTEEN

A SECOND CHANCE

The play-by-play announcer stammered as he interrupted a football game between the New York Giants and a short-lived team called the Brooklyn Dodgers. "The Japanese have attacked Pearl Harbor, Hawaii, by air, President Roosevelt just announced," he said, his voice rebounding throughout the stadium on the blustery afternoon of December 7, 1941. Throughout the announced crowd of 55,501, young men stood up and made their way to the exits, preparing to report for duty.

The reality of another world war fell on the city like a sudden rain. At the Brooklyn Navy Yard, heavily armed guards set up checkpoints at the dry docks where two 45,000-ton battleships were under construction. Police officers surrounded the Japanese consulate on Fifth Avenue, where they could detect the smell of burning paper. Fighter planes from Long Island's Mitchel Field hummed along the shoreline.

There was a sense that the enemy could appear at any moment, re-creating the terror of Pearl Harbor along Park Avenue or the Brooklyn Promenade. Two weeks later, *LIFE* magazine published a detailed sketch showing a squadron of Nazi aircraft approaching the city from the southeast, under the headline "How Nazi Planes May Bomb New York."

In those early days of the war, an invasion seemed inevitable. Throughout the country, Americans began the glum process of boarding up and hiding the objects that mattered most. Workers at the Museum of Modern Art in New York began pulling down paintings from the third-floor galleries and putting them in a sandbagged storeroom each night before rehanging them each morning. On the Upper East Side, the Frick Collection painted its skylights black. Museum workers across the city received memos sent out by building engineers on how to respond in the event of a bombing. In the case of an attack, workers should immediately head to the exhibition floors and "gather up shattered fragments [of an artwork] and wrap [them] in cloth marked with collection number." To ready itself for a sustained bombing of the city, the American Museum of Natural History developed plans to turn its complex of buildings into a vast public shelter, going so far as to make a deal to purchase pianos in bulk to entertain and calm those it expected to host huddled inside.

Priceless pieces of art and culture were nailed into crates and rushed away from the coasts. Seventy-five of the most important paintings and sculptures in the collection of the National Gallery of Art were loaded onto a train and sent to storage at the sprawling Biltmore estate, the largest private home in the country, tucked in the mountains near Asheville, North Carolina. Some fifteen thousand items from the Metropolitan Museum of Art, filling up ninety truckloads, were hidden at an empty mansion outside Philadelphia.

At the American Museum of Natural History, the size and

weight of most objects on display made the question of hiding them impossible. One dinosaur specimen alone could fill up more than a dozen truckloads, making a wholesale evacuation of the collection the size and scope of a military operation. The museum packed up precious materials such as gold and diamonds that were easy to transport. But the dinosaur collection remained in place, ready to brave whatever the war brought.

All except for one. Since Brown found the first *T. rex* nearly thirty-five years earlier, no one else had duplicated his feat. The three *T. rex* specimens in the American Museum remained the only relics of the creature known to science. Should the museum suffer a hit during a raid in New York, all evidence of the world's most recognizable dinosaur could be lost. Fifteen boxes of bones containing the first *T. rex* uncovered in Hell Creek soon arrived at the Carnegie Museum in Pittsburgh, which had agreed to purchase the specimen for roughly $100,000 in today's dollars. The sale of the priceless *T. rex* holotype—the term given to the first example of any species found—to a rival institution would have been inconceivable a generation earlier, but the animosity between the two museums had faded.

Osborn had died in 1935—living just long enough to praise the rise of Nazism in Europe and Hitler's attempts at putting the racist eugenics principles he endorsed into practice. He retired on January 1, 1933, as the most powerful person the American Museum had ever known, twenty-five years after assuming its presidency. In that time, he sent expeditions to every continent on the globe, authored more than one hundred scientific papers, planned a grand new museum entrance on Central Park West in honor of his childhood friend Theodore Roosevelt, and increased the museum's endowment by nearly $200 million in today's dollars. Yet it was in ways unlikely to be noticed by a visitor that his influence was most greatly felt. For a generation, every display and exhibit he approved was infected by his opinion that racial hierarchy was a scientific fact.

Thanks largely to its collection of dinosaurs—especially the world's only *T. rex*—the American Museum had become *the* destination for millions of school-aged children. And all those visitors were indoctrinated into Osborn's worldview without even being aware of what they were absorbing—a worldview that curators at the museum today are still working to remove from its displays. The final years of Osborn's life were consumed with his search for the origin of what he called the white race and his fear that it would be extinguished. At a time when science was often used to backstop racism, the intensity of Osborn's vitriol was noted by his peers.

As New York prepared for a possible German attack, Brown was among the last people at the museum who remembered the cowboys and prospectors whose work filled its shelves and the race between museums to find and display the most impressive dinosaurs. When the Carnegie Museum unveiled the specimen it purchased from the American Museum in a "Godzilla pose" in 1942, it was the first time in 66 million years that a *T. rex* stood in any place other than New York City. The local press boasted of the museum's "new baby," calling it "the more spectacular of all the exhibits in the Gallery of Fossil Reptiles." The same year, Brown turned sixty-five, the mandatory age for retirement at the institution where he had worked since he was in college. Out of respect for his contributions he was given the title Curator

Emeritus and an office—his last connections to the only job he had ever known.

Brown was not built to slow down. Even well into his fifties, he had embarked on expeditions that left others struggling to keep up. For company, he'd often brought along his second wife, a New York socialite and author named Lilian McLaughlin, whom he'd married in 1922. Brash and accustomed to the spotlight, Lilian was the opposite of his first wife, Marion, in nearly every way. Yet in her love of attention she was more like her husband than he perhaps recognized. Together, they'd trekked through Asia, their path dictated by the needs of the museum. In Pakistan, Brown attempted to find the remains of an animal now known as *Paraceratherium*, an early rhinoceros that was among the largest land mammals to have ever lived. In central Burma, he'd disappeared for several days in the jungle after missing a fork in the trail and discovered a glowing spider that darted away when he tried to grab it.

A bout of malaria that had left Brown with a fever of 106.2 degrees was among the few things that could stop him. Lilian had packed him in a bathtub full of ice and administered massive doses of quinine as he rambled in delusions. "It was mostly of his youth that he spoke. Sometimes he was a small boy again, wandering over the coal mounds on his father's Kansas farm, collecting his first precious specimens," she wrote in a memoir of their adventures titled *I Married a Dinosaur*. After six days, the fever broke. A shell of his former self, Brown weighed less than a hundred pounds and was too weak to walk more than a few paces. Yet within a few weeks, he was strolling through a nearby garden.

"Before we knew it, the man was dressing in his new Palm Beach suit and wanting to go places," Lilian wrote.

Not long after they were married, Brown took Lilian on a private tour of the dinosaur halls, where, "when Barnum explained them, speaking as one would of old friends, [the specimens] seemed to change and warm into life," Lilian wrote. "And suddenly it dawned on me as never before why my husband was so obsessed with his work. It was a great work. He had done this. The amassing of these prehistoric wonders had been chiefly his doing, and it was not a small thing."

The drive to do great work did not go away with age. A few months after his retirement in the summer of 1942, Brown received a call from Col. William J. Donovan, chief of the newly created Office of Strategic Services, the forerunner of the modern Central Intelligence Agency. Donovan's network of more than twelve thousand people was working to prepare occupied Europe for the eventual landing of American soldiers. He asked Brown for help in planning a possible invasion route via the Aegean Sea, based on Brown's experience prospecting for fossils in the region. Brown jumped at the chance for another adventure. He left Lilian at their apartment on Broadway, around the corner from the museum, and rushed to wartime Washington, where he spent his days detailing the geological formations and features of the Greek islands.

There was no time for him to find his own place to live in D.C., so he moved in with the person he had been avoiding for much of her life: his daughter, Frances. It was the first and only time that the pair had lived together since she was an infant. She had been in Washington for over a year, working in the editorial office of the American Red Cross, after the junior college where she taught English literature for seven years closed due to the war. When they stood next to each other, the physical resemblance between the two was undeniable. Frances shared her father's soft eyes, round face, and lips that turned up at the edges, as if always ready to break out in a laugh. Beyond appearance, she was in nearly every way his opposite. Where he once jumped aboard a boat to Patagonia with two hours' notice, she was always on time for choir practice. Where he delighted in breaking rules, her job as a college dean was to enforce them.

Like her mother before her, Frances slowly found herself swept up in her father's energy. Each day would be filled with work. Then each night was filled with a sense of possibility. One

In 1934, Brown discovered one of the most important fossil sites in North America. Known as the Howe Quarry, Brown and his team—shown here—found more than 4,000 fossil bones in just six months.

night they would go to a party, the next a concert, and then a reception the following evening only to repeat the cycle again, a storm with Brown always at its center. It was as if Frances had opened her home to a twentysomething, not a semi-retired, weathered man.

Like all of Brown's adventures, his time in Washington was short-lived. He spent less than twelve months in the capital before joining the Board of Economic Warfare in 1943, where he turned his attention to completing an aerial survey of Alberta to locate potential oil fields. By the time he returned to work for the military searching for signs of enemy camouflage in the spy photographs taken over areas in Africa, India, and the Mediterranean islands

Brown often worked alone during the early days of his career. But as he aged, he often had a team of assistants with him in the field who all had specialized jobs.

where he had once prospected, Frances had left Washington for a job at another college.

Though brief, the time spent in his daughter's company finally opened Brown up to their relationship. He brought her along on expeditions to Guatemala and Montana, showing her what she had been missing while in the care of her grandparents as a young girl. In the final years of his life, Frances became one of Brown's closest confidantes. In 1962, the Sinclair Refining Company asked Brown, then eighty-nine years old, to supervise the construction of nine life-size fiberglass dinosaurs planned for its Dinoland exhibition at the 1964 World's Fair. Fifty million people were expected to attend. Brown commuted daily by limousine from Manhattan to Hudson, New York, to ensure that

Even as he got older Brown continued to work in the field despite the often-punishing heat and terrain. Here, he excavates a fossil in Big Bend, Texas, in 1940.

Though he loved to work in the field most of all, Brown enjoyed walking the halls of the American Museum as he got older and watching how visitors enjoyed his discoveries. In this 1938 photo, he is showing a set of dinosaur tracks to a group of students.

the anatomy of each specimen was accurate. It seemed only fitting that a man so connected to the deep past would play a small part in a celebration of the future. "This was sheer joy for him. Who else at eighty-nine years of age could command an important, new job?" Frances wrote.

As he rode each day along the Hudson River, he often had Frances at his side. Their conversations ranged widely, touching on everything from proposed modifications to the exhibition's plans to how the models would be loaded on a raft to take them to Queens, to any new idea that he had. But those details often drifted away as Frances got lost in her father's stories from his life in the prospecting fields.

Brown did not live to see his dinosaurs delight the city that had made his dreams possible. Two weeks before his ninetieth birthday, he laid down his fork at the dinner table and told Lilian that he was very tired. He slipped into a coma that night and never recovered, dying in St. Luke's Hospital on February 5, 1963. He was buried in Oxford, New York, next to his first wife, Marion. His death was noted in a short article in the *New York Times*. "Dr. Brown was a tireless fossil hunter and was known as the Father of the Dinosaurs because of his successes during the nearly seven decades in which he served the museum," the paper read, a eulogy that Brown would no doubt have enjoyed, given his difficulties in completing a doctorate at Columbia.

During his life, Brown was widely recognized as the best dinosaur collector who ever lived. He went out into the unknown and came back with new puzzle pieces that told the story of life on Earth. And he did it again and again and again, a run of success and discovery as impressive as navigating the stars. At his death, more than half of the dinosaur specimens on exhibit at the American Museum of Natural History were the result of his work, a priceless collection that turned it from an afterthought into one of the most vital museums in the world. "He has discovered many of the most important and most spectacular specimens in the whole history of paleontology," a fellow collector, Roy Chapman Andrew, wrote in a foreword to Lilian Brown's first book. "When he ceases to look for bones on this earth, the celestial fossil fields may well prepare for a thorough inspection by his all-seeing eyes. He'll arrive in the Other World with a pick, shellack, and plaster or else he won't go."

Brown helped fill the halls of the American Museum of Natural History with dinosaur fossils.

The New York World's Fair opened on April 22, 1964, a little more than a year after Brown's death. Visitors who walked the grounds in Queens could catch a glimpse of the first Ford Mustang, ride on a Ferris wheel in the shape of a giant tire, or try to get the song from Disney's "It's a Small World" ride out of their heads. For a brief moment, it was as if P. T. Barnum's dime museum had been reborn for the modern age. And in the middle of the fair, staring directly at the giant Ferris wheel, stood a twenty-foot-tall celebrity. Fifty-nine years after Barnum Brown first uncovered it in the Montana Badlands, a modern monster reigned in the shadow of the Manhattan skyline: *Tyrannosaurus rex.*

Epilogue

THE MONSTER'S TRACKS

*T*yrannosaurus rex remains surprisingly alive for a creature that went extinct 66 million years ago. Researchers studying the animal now know that, far from being lumbering brutes, T. rex were intelligent creatures that lived in complex social systems. They were blessed with oversized nostrils and eyes and an outsized brain case that likely gave them a superb sense of sight and smell, fashioning them into formidable hunters at a time when the Earth's temperatures were near their highest in known history.

Paleontologists now believe that 20,000 adult T. rex lived in North America at any one time. Over the 2.4 million years the species was in existence, a total of some 2.5 billion adult T. rex walked the Earth. Paleontologists now estimate that only 1 out of every 80 million T. rex that ever lived was fossilized. Given that there have only been about fifty T. rex specimens ever found, Brown's discovery of three of them becomes all the more astounding!

It's fair to wonder how much of the history of life on this planet would remain unknown today had Barnum Brown never escaped the life that was set out for him on his family farm. What would a modern world without a T. rex look like? It's easy to list the billions of dollars in movie box-office receipts that were brought in by the appearance of a snarling T. rex, the countless children's toys and pajamas with the dinosaur's image, the tourist attractions ranging from roadside fossil digs in Montana to roller coasters named after the planet's most ferocious beast—all of which would be lost. And every child who attends a natural history museum on a field trip has Barnum Brown—and the *T. rex*—to thank.

Yet its influence is greater than that. Without the *T. rex*, it's likely that dinosaurs would have remained little more than novelties. They would never have inspired the public and scientists alike to imagine prehistoric Earth as a complex former world or prompted them to search the past for clues on how a rapidly changing climate once upended the dominant species of the prehistoric past. As temperatures continue to rise today, we can look at the fossils of a *T. rex* and see a glimpse of what may become of humankind if we do not take more steps to address the climate crisis. In the end, that could be the most important lesson we can draw from the fearsome reign of the *T. rex*: in the battle for life on Earth, the climate always wins.

The animal at the intersection of popular culture and modern science still stands on the fourth floor of a museum in Manhattan on the edge of Central Park. There, visitors find themselves gazing across a 66-million-year gap at the greatest predator that nature ever produced—and whose discovery was the greatest legacy of a man who could not be contained.

Acknowledgments

Escaping into dinosaur digs in Montana—or at least pretending to—while working on this book was a welcome diversion as the coronavirus raced through New York City and its suburbs, an area that I now call home. Though libraries were closed and trips into the field canceled, a number of people continued to go out of their way to assist me in my attempt to tell the story of Barnum Brown and the monster he found.

The staff at the American Museum of Natural History were unfailingly helpful and courteous as I came back again and again with questions. Chief among them was Susan Bell, who opened the museum's archives for me and spent several long afternoons in a stuffy records room located in the building's attic while I paged through Barnum Brown's papers and mice scurried past our feet. Dr. Mark Norrell, who, with Dr. Lowell Dingus, wrote a fantastic biography of Barnum Brown, extended his help in finding documents for my own work. And Matt Heenan, in the museum's business office, made the process of finding and republishing photographs from the American Museum's archives incredibly easy.

I would also like to thank several scholars whose work was invaluable to this project. Paul Brinkman uncovered a treasure trove of details of what he called the Second Jurassic Dinosaur Rush, while Lukas Rieppel artfully examined how dinosaur fossils became a status symbol for Gilded Age tycoons. Adrienne Mayor's work into how folklore incorporated fossils, meanwhile, helped provide a grounding for how humans interacted with dinosaurs before the advent of formalized science, and Deborah Cadbury's book *The Dinosaur Hunters* helped flesh out the stories of early fossil hunters in England.

I am exceedingly fortunate to once again work with a team at W. W. Norton that was supportive of this project from the beginning and continued to make it better every step of the way. My editor, Jill Bialosky, pushed me to go deeper into Brown's character and offered innumerable suggestions along the way, which helped me get over whatever obstacle was in front of me. I am thankful that Emily Easton helped refashion this book for young readers, and to Kristin Allard and Rachelle Mandik for ensuring that it remained accurate. Hana Nakamura conceived of a brilliant book jacket design, while Louise Brockett conjured the perfect subtitle.

Special thanks also go to Larry Weissman and Sasha Alper, who helped shape this book back when it was just the wisp of an idea and wouldn't rest until we got its wording just right, and Josie Freedman at CAA.

I am also fortunate to benefit from the support and company of Alan Yang, Jennifer Ablan, Lauren Young, Megan Davies, Dan Burns, Helen Coster, Sam Mamudi, Felix Gillette, John and Carol Ordover, Tony and Maryanne Petrizio, Robert, Gina and Gary Scott, Emily Davis and Ryan and Diane Randall.

And finally, infinite love and thanks go to Megan, Henry, and Isla Randall, who made every day a good one regardless of how overwhelming the process of writing a book can sometimes feel. I am incredibly lucky to have you in my life.

Selected Bibliography and Sources

Prologue: The Center of the World

Davey, Colin. *The American Museum of Natural History and How It Got That Way.* New York: Empire States Editions, 2019.

Preston, Douglas. *Dinosaurs in the Attic.* New York: St. Martin's Griffin, 1993.

Wilford, John Noble. "When Humans Became Human." *New York Times*, February 26, 2002.

Chapter One: A Life That Could Contain Him

Brown, Barnum. Unpublished notes. American Museum of Natural History Vertebrate Paleontology Archives.

Brown, Frances R. *Let's Call Him Barnum.* New York: Vantage Press, 1987.

Cadbury, Deborah. *The Dinosaur Hunters.* London: Foulsham, 2000.

Dingus, Lowell, and Mark A. Norell. *Barnum Brown: The Man Who Discovered T. Rex.* Berkeley: University of California Press, 2010.

Rabbitt, Mary C. "The United States Geological Survey: 1879–1989." *U.S. Geological Survey Circular.* Washington, D.C.: Government Printing Office, 1984.

Thomson, Keith S. "Marginalia: Vestiges of James Hutton." *American Scientist* 89, no. 3.

Chapter Two: A World Before Ours

Bailey, E.H.S. "Samuel Wendell Williston: A Kansas Tribute." *Sigma Xi Quarterly* 7, no. 1 (1919).

Brinkman, Paul. *The Second Jurassic Dinosaur Rush.* Chicago: University of Chicago Press, 2010.

Brown, Barnum. Unpublished notes. American Museum of Natural History Vertebrate Paleontology Archives.

Cadbury, Deborah. *The Dinosaur Hunters.* London: Foulsham, 2000.

Conniff, Richard. *House of Lost Worlds: Dinosaurs, Dynasties, and the Story of Life on Earth.* New Haven: Yale University Press, 2016.

Cordley, Richard. *A History of Lawrence, Kansas: From the First Settlement to the Close of the Rebellion.* Lawrence Journal Press, 1895.

Davidson, Jane P. *The Bone Sharp: The Life of Edward Drinker Cope.* Philadelphia: Academy of Natural Sciences Philadelphia, 1997.

Dean, Dennis. *Gideon Mantell and the Discovery of Dinosaurs.* Cambridge: Cambridge University Press, 1999.

Dwight, Timothy. *Memories of Yale Life and Men, 1854–1899.* New York: Dodd, Mead, 1903.

Jaffe, Mark. *The Gilded Dinosaur: The Fossil War Between E. D. Cope and O. C. Marsh and the Rise of American Science.* New York: Crown, 2000.

Kolbert, Elizabeth. "The Lost World." *The New Yorker*, December 8, 2013.

———. *The Sixth Extinction: An Unnatural History.* New York: Henry Holt and Co., 2014.

Mayor, Adrienne. *The First Fossil Hunters: Paleontology in Greek and Roman Times.* Princeton: Princeton University Press, 2000.

Murray, J. *Report of the Eleventh Meeting of the British Association for the Advancement of Science.* 1842.

———. *Fossil Legends of the First Americans.* Princeton: Princeton University Press, 2013.

Owen, Rev. Richard. *The Life of Richard Owen.* Vol. 1. London, Gregg International, 1894.

Pierce, Patricia. *Jurassic Mary: Mary Anning and the Primeval Monsters*. London: History Press, 2015.

Wallis, Severn Teackle. *Discourse on the Life and Character of George Peabody*. Baltimore: John Murphy & Co., 1870.

Winchell, N. H., ed. *The American Geologist: A Monthly Journal of Geology and Allied Sciences*. Minneapolis: Geological Publishing Company, 1899.

Chapter Three: Scraping the Surface

Brinkman, Paul. *The Second Jurassic Dinosaur Rush*. Chicago: University of Chicago Press, 2010.

Brown, Barnum. Unpublished notes. American Museum of Natural History Vertebrate Paleontology Archives.

Dingus, Lowell, and Mark A. Norell. *Barnum Brown: The Man Who Discovered T. Rex*. Berkeley: University of California Press, 2010.

Dodson, Peter. *The Horned Dinosaurs: A Natural History*. Princeton: Princeton University Press, 2017.

Marsh, O. C. "Notice of New American Dinosauria." *American Journal of Science* (1889).

Chapter Four: Creatures Equally Colossal and Equally Strange

Cain, Victoria. "Albert Bickmore." *Harvard Magazine*, September–October 2008.

Chamberlain, Joshua Lawrence. *Universities and Their Sons: History, Influence and Characteristics of American Universities, with Biographical Sketches and Portraits of Alumni and Recipients of Honorary Degrees*. Vol. 1. Boston: R. Herndon Co., 1898.

de Chadarevian, Doraya, and Nick Hopwood. *Models: The Third Dimension of Science*. Palo Alto: Stanford University Press, 2004.

Dingus, Lowell, and Mark A. Norell. *Barnum Brown: The Man Who Discovered T. Rex*. Berkeley: University of California Press, 2010.

Gregory, William K. *Biographical Memoir of Henry Fairfield Osborn*. 1936.

Peck, Robert McCracken. "The Art of Bones." *Natural History*. May 10, 2012.

Proceedings of the Academy of Natural Sciences of Philadelphia 21. Philadelphia, 1869.

Proceedings of the American Association for the Advancement of Science 47. Salem, 1898.

Rainger, Ronald. *An Agenda for Antiquity: Henry Fairfield Osborn and Vertebrate Paleontology at the American Museum of Natural History, 1890–1935*. Birmingham: University of Alabama Press, 1991.

Regal, Brian. *Henry Fairfield Osborn: Race and the Search for the Origins of Man*. London: Routledge, 2002.

Scott, William Berryman. *Some Memories of a Paleontologist*. New York: Forgotten Books, 2017 (reprint).

Smith, Phillip. *The Popular History of England from the Earliest Times to the Year 1848*. London: A. Fullerton & Co., 1883.

Twelfth Annual Report of the Board of Commissioners of the Central Park, for the Year Ending December 31, 1868. New York: Evening Post Seam Presses, 1867.

Chapter Five: Empty Rooms

Ayres, James J. *Gold and Sunshine: Reminiscences of Early California*. Boston: Gorham Press, 1922.

Barnum, P. T. *Struggles and Triumphs: Or, Forty Years' Recollections of P. T. Barnum, Written by Himself*. Hartford: J. B. Burr and Co., 1869.

Hermann, A. "Modern Laboratory Methods in Vertebrate Paleontology." *Bulletin of the American Museum of Natural History* 26 (1909).

Kohlstedt, Sally Gregory. "Curiosities and Cabinets: Natural History Museums and Education on the Antebellum Campus." *Isis* 79, no. 3 (1988).

New York Times. "Disastrous Fire: Total Destruction of Barnum's American Museum." July 14, 1865.

Rainger, Ronald. *An Agenda for Antiquity: Henry Fairfield Osborn and Vertebrate Paleontology at the American Museum of Natural History, 1890–1935.* Birmingham: University of Alabama Press, 1991.

Rieppel, Lukas. *Assembling the Dinosaur: Fossil Hunters, Tycoons, and the Making of a Spectacle.* Cambridge, MA: Harvard University Press, 2019.

Ross, Delaney. "150-Year-Old Diorama Surprises Scientists with Human Remains." *National Geographic,* January 29, 2017.

Sellers, Charles Coleman. "The Peale Portraits of Benjamin Franklin." *Proceedings of the American Philosophical Society* 94, no 3 (1950).

Stulman Dennett, Andrea. *Weird and Wonderful: The Dime Museum in America.* New York: New York University Press, 1997.

Chapter Six: A Real Adventure

Brown, Barnum. Unpublished notes. American Museum of Natural History Vertebrate Paleontology Archives.

Dingus, Lowell, and Mark A. Norell. *Barnum Brown: The Man Who Discovered T. Rex.* Berkeley: University of California Press, 2010.

Rainger, Ronald. "Collectors and Entrepreneurs: Hatcher, Wortman, and the Structure of American Vertebrate Paleontology Circa 1900." *Earth Sciences History* 9, no. 1 (1990).

Rieppel, Lukas. *Assembling the Dinosaur: Fossil Hunters, Tycoons, and the Making of a Spectacle.* Cambridge, MA: Harvard University Press, 2019.

Thomson, Kenneth. *The Legacy of the Mastodon: The Golden Age of Fossils in America.* New Haven: Yale University Press, 2008.

Wortman, J. L. "Restoration of Oxyaena lupina Copa, With Descriptions of Certain New Species of Eocene Creodonts." *Bulletin of the American Museum of Natural History* 12–13 (1900).

Chapter Seven: Finding a Place in the World

Annual Report of the American Museum of Natural History, vols. 29–32.

Brown, Frances R. *Let's Call Him Barnum.* New York: Vantage Press, 1987.

Dingus, Lowell, and Mark A. Norell. *Barnum Brown: The Man Who Discovered T. Rex.* Berkeley: University of California Press, 2010.

Duffus, R. L. *Lillian Wald: Neighbor and Crusader.* New York: Macmillan, 1939.

Jackson, Kenneth T., and David S. Dunbar. *Empire City: New York Through the Centuries.* New York: Columbia University Press, 2002.

Riis, Jacob. *How the Other Half Lives: Studies Among the Tenements of New York.* New York: Penguin Classics, 1997 (reprint).

Chapter Eight: The Most Extreme Place on Earth

Brown, Barnum. Unpublished notes. American Museum of Natural History Vertebrate Paleontology Archives.

Brown, Frances R. *Let's Call Him Barnum.* New York: Vantage Press, 1987.

Brown, Janet. *Charles Darwin: The Power of Place.* New York: Knopf, 2003.

Cope, E. D. "Review: Ameghino on the Extinct Mammalia of Argentina." *American Naturalist* 25, no. 296 (August 1891).

Dana, Richard Henry, Jr. *Two Years Before the Mast.* New York: Signet, 2009 (reprint).

Dingus, Lowell. *King of the Dinosaur Hunters: The Life of John Bell Hatcher and the Discoveries that Shaped Paleontology*. New York: Pegasus Books, 2018.

Dingus, Lowell, and Mark A. Norell. *Barnum Brown: The Man Who Discovered T. Rex*. Berkeley: University of California Press, 2010.

Gabriel, M. S. "Ota Benga Having a Fine Time: A Visitor at the Zoo Finds No Reason for Protests About the Pygmy." *New York Times*, September 13, 1906.

Keller, Mitch. "The Scandal at the Zoo." *New York Times*, August 6, 2006.

Larkum, Anthony W. D., ed. *A Natural Calling: Life, Letters and Diaries of Charles Darwin and William Darwin Fox*. New York: Springer Science and Business Media, 2009.

Meacham, Steve. "Forgotten Death at Sea Stoked Darwin's Success." *Sydney Morning Herald*, June 27, 2009.

Chapter Nine: Big Things

Batz, Bob Jr. "Dippy the Star-Spangled Dinosaur." *Pittsburgh Post–Gazette*, July 2, 1999.

Brinkman, Paul. *The Second Jurassic Dinosaur Rush*. Chicago: University of Chicago Press, 2010.

Brown, Barnum. Unpublished notes. American Museum of Natural History Vertebrate Paleontology Archives.

Nasaw, David. *Andrew Carnegie*. New York: Penguin, 2007.

Rea, Tom. *Bone Wars: The Excavation and Celebrity of Andrew Carnegie's Dinosaur*. Pittsburgh: University of Pittsburgh Press, 2004.

Rieppel, Lukas. *Assembling the Dinosaur: Fossil Hunters, Tycoons, and the Making of a Spectacle*. Cambridge, MA: Harvard University Press, 2019.

Wister, Owen. *The Virginian: A Horseman of the Plains*. New York: Macmillan, 1904.

Chapter Ten: A Very Costly Season

Annual Report of the American Museum of Natural History, vols. 30–35.

Brinkman, Paul. *The Second Jurassic Dinosaur Rush*. Chicago: University of Chicago Press, 2010.

Brown, Barnum. Unpublished notes. American Museum of Natural History Vertebrate Paleontology Archives.

Dingus, Lowell, and Mark A. Norell. *Barnum Brown: The Man Who Discovered T. Rex*. Berkeley: University of California Press, 2010.

Chapter Eleven: The Bones of the King

Annual Report of the American Museum of Natural History, 1903.

Brown, Barnum. Unpublished notes. American Museum of Natural History Vertebrate Paleontology Archives.

Browne, John. *Seven Elements That Changed the World*. New York: Open Road Media, 2014.

Dingus, Lowell. *Hell Creek, Montana: America's Key to the Prehistoric Past*. New York: St. Martin's, 2015.

Dingus, Lowell, and Mark A. Norell. *Barnum Brown: The Man Who Discovered T. Rex*. Berkeley: University of California Press, 2010.

Gedden, Stanley. *Big Bone Lick: The Cradle of American Paleontology*. Lexington, KY: University of Kentucky Press, 2021.

Gray, Christopher. "Streetscapes: The Dorilton; A Blowzy 1902 Broadway Belle." *New York Times*, September 30, 1990.

The Horseless Age: The Automobile Trade Magazine, February 19, 1902.

Lewis, Meriwether, and William C. Clark. *Original Journals of the Lewis and Clark Expedition, 1804–1806*. New York: Dodd, Mead, 1904.

Chapter Twelve: New Beginnings

Black, Riley. "Everything You Wanted to Know About Dinosaur Sex." *Smithsonian*, February 10, 2011.

Brown, Barnum. Unpublished notes. American Museum of Natural History Vertebrate Paleontology Archives.

Brown, Frances R. *Let's Call Him Barnum*. New York: Vantage Press, 1987.

Moore, Randy. *Dinosaurs by the Decades*. Santa Barbara, CA: Greenwood, 2014.

Norman, Andrew. *Charles Darwin: Destroyer of Myths*. New York: Skyhorse, 2014.

Osborn, Henry Fairfield. "Tyrannosaurus and Other Cretaceous Carnivorous Dinosaurs." *Bulletin of the American Museum of Natural History* 21 (1905).

Rieppel, Lukas. "Bringing Dinosaurs Back to Life: Exhibiting Prehistory at the American Museum of Natural History." *Isis* 103, no. 3 (September 2012).

"Sir Edwin Ray Lankester." *Nature* 159, 734 (May 31, 1947).

Sullivan, Jill A. *Popular Exhibitions, Science and Showmanship, 1840–1910*. London: Routledge, 2015.

Wellnhofer, Peter. "Archaeopteryx." *Scientific American* 262, no. 5 (May 1990).

Chapter Thirteen: The Hardest Work He Could Find

Brown, Barnum. Unpublished notes. American Museum of Natural History Vertebrate Paleontology Archives.

Brown, Frances R. *Let's Call Him Barnum*. New York: Vantage Press, 1987.

Dingus, Lowell, and Mark A. Norell. *Barnum Brown: The Man Who Discovered T. Rex*. Berkeley: University of California Press, 2010.

New York Times. "The Prize Fighter of Antiquity Discovered and Restored." December 30, 1906.

Chapter Fourteen: A New World

Brown, Barnum. Unpublished notes. American Museum of Natural History Vertebrate Paleontology Archives.

Brown, Frances R. *Let's Call Him Barnum*. New York: Vantage Press, 1987.

Canemaker, John. *Winsor McCay: His Life and Art*. Boca Raton, FL: CRC Press, 2018.

Dickerson, Mary Cynthia, ed. *Natural History: The Journal of the American Museum of Natural History*. Volume 20. New York City: The American Museum of Natural History, 1920.

Dingus, Lowell, and Mark A. Norell. *Barnum Brown: The Man Who Discovered T. Rex*. Berkeley: University of California Press, 2010.

Doyle, Arthur Conan. *The Lost World*. New York: A. L. Burt Co., 1912.

Eugenics, Genetics and the Family: Scientific Papers of the Second International Congress of Eugenics, Held at the American Museum of Natural History, New York. September 22–28, 1921. Vol. 1

Prothero, Donald R. *The Story of the Dinosaurs in 25 Discoveries: Amazing Fossils and the People Who Found Them*. New York: Columbia University Press, 2019.

Purdy, Jedediah. "Environmentalism's Racist History." *New Yorker*, August 13, 2015.

Sternberg, Charles Hazelius. *The Life of a Fossil Hunter*. New York: H. Holt, 1909.

Chapter Fifteen: The Monster Unveiled

Annual Report of the American Museum of Natural History, 1949.

Brown, Frances R. *Let's Call Him Barnum*. New York: Vantage Press, 1987.

Dingus, Lowell, and Mark A. Norell. *Barnum Brown: The Man Who Discovered T. Rex.* Berkeley: University of California Press, 2010.

Hall, Mordaunt. "The Screen; A Wonderful Farce." *New York Times,* February 9, 1925.

———. "A Fantastic Film in Which a Monstrous Ape Uses Automobiles for Missiles and Climbs a Skyscraper." *New York Times,* March 3, 1933.

National Army Museum. "Battle of Loos." Accessed at nam.ac.uk/explore/battle-loos.

New York Times. "It's the Red Sox Again and Again It's 2 to 1." October 9, 1915.

Paul, Gregory S. "The Art of Charles R. Knight." *Scientific American* 274, no. 6 (June 1996).

Chapter Sixteen: A Second Chance

Brown, Barnum. "A Luminous Spider." *Science* 62, no. 1599 (August 21, 1925).

Brown, Frances R. *Let's Call Him Barnum.* New York: Vantage Press, 1987.

Brown, Lilian. *I Married a Dinosaur.* Landisville, PA: Coachwhip, 2010 (reprint).

Dingus, Lowell, and Mark A. Norell. *Barnum Brown: The Man Who Discovered T. Rex.* Berkeley: University of California Press, 2010.

Jamieson, Wendell. "The Panic After Pearl Harbor: NYC on the Cusp of WW2." *New York Daily News,* August 14, 2017.

Keith, Sir Arthur. "Whence Came the White Race?" *New York Times,* October 12, 1930.

Macdonald, William. "Mr. Grant's Plea for a Nordic, Protestant America." *New York Times,* November, 5, 1933.

New York Times. "Barnum Brown Dies at 89; Noted Collector of Fossils." February 6, 1963.

New York Times. "Birth Control Peril to Race, Says Osborn." August 23, 1932.

Nicholas, Lynn H. *The Rape of Europe: The Fate of Europe's Treasures in the Third Reich and the Second World War.* New York: Knopf Doubleday, 2009.

Shirley, Craig. *December, 1941: 31 Days That Changed America and Saved the World.* Nashville: Thomas Nelson, 2011.

Sports Illustrated. "The Day War Came to the Polo Grounds." October 24, 1966.

Epilogue: The Monster's Tracks

Browne, Malcolm W. "Tyrannosaurus Skeleton Is Sold to a Museum for $8.36 Million." *New York Times,* October 5, 1997.

Chang, Kenneth. "How Many Tyrannosaurus Rexes Ever Lived on Earth? Here's a New Clue." *New York Times,* April 15, 2021.

Christies. "The Life and Times of Stan, One of the Most Complete T. Rex Skeletons Ever Found." Christie's online catalog. Accessed at https://www.christies.com/features/The-life-of-STAN-a-T-rex-excavated-in-1992-10872-$2aspx.

Freedom du Lac, J. "The T. Rex that Got Away." *Washington Post,* April 5, 2014.

Gorman, James. "Tyrannosaurus Rex: The Once and Future King." *New York Times,* March 4, 2019.

Holson, Laura M. "He Listed a T. Rex Fossil on eBay for $2.95 Million. Scientists Weren't Thrilled." *New York Times,* April 17, 2019.

———. "'Scotty' the T. Rex Is the Heaviest Ever Found, Scientists Say." *New York Times,* March 28, 2019.

Small, Zachary. "A T. Rex Skeleton Arrives in Rockefeller Center Ahead of Auction." *New York Times,* September 16, 2020.

———. "T. Rex Skeleton Brings $31.8 Million at Christie's Auction." *New York Times,* October 6, 2020.

Index

Page numbers in **bold** have pictures.